# GOLF
## MAGAZINE

# *The Best*
# PUTTING
# INSTRUCTION
# BOOK EVER!

A SPORTS ILLUSTRATED PUBLICATION

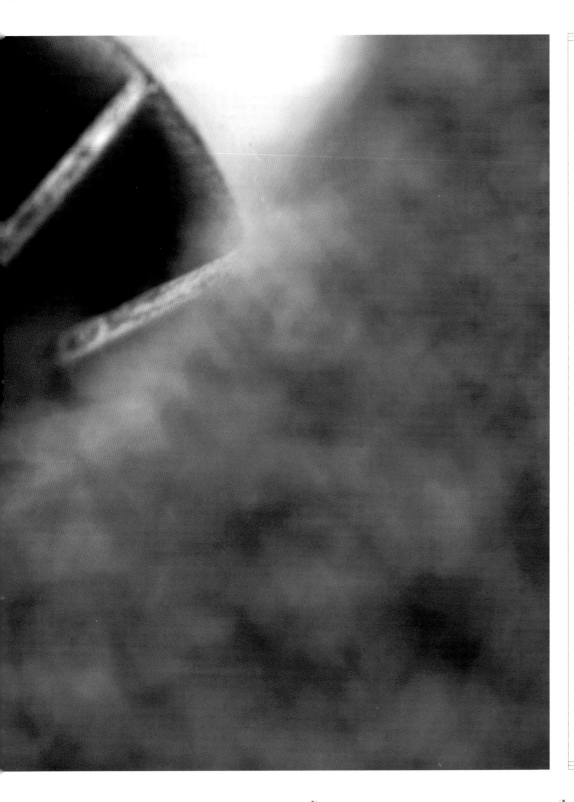

© 2010 Time Home Entertainment Inc.

Published by Time Home Entertainment Inc.
135 West 50th Street
New York, New York 10020

Some of the material in this book was
previously published in *Golf Magazine*, and
is reprinted with permission by Time Inc.

ISBN 10: 1-60320-148-3
ISBN 13: 978-1-60320-148-3
Library of Congress Control Number:
2010927618

Printed in China

We welcome your comments and suggestions
about Time Home Entertainment Inc. Books.
Please write to us at:
Time Home Entertainment Inc. Books
Attention: Book Editors
PO Box 11016
Des Moines, IA 50336-1016

If you would like to order any of our
hardcover Collector's Edition books,
please call us at
1-800-327-6388. (Monday through Friday,
7:00 a.m.- 8:00 p.m.; Saturday, 7:00 a.m.-
6:00 p.m. Central Time).

Cover/book design: Paul Ewen
Cover photography: Angus Murray

# GOLF
## MAGAZINE

## *The Best*
# PUTTING
# INSTRUCTION
# BOOK EVER!

The 10 Brightest Minds in Putting Show You the Easy Way to
Make the Hole Look Bigger and Sink More Putts

EDITED BY DAVID DeNUNZIO

**WITH THE
TOP 100 TEACHERS
IN AMERICA**

A SPORTS ILLUSTRATED PUBLICATION

# Your Guide to the Ultimate Putting Experience

It's called the *Best Putting Instruction Book Ever!* for a reason: It's written by the strongest collection of putting instructors and researchers the golf world has ever seen

**P**utting is an enigma. It defines greatness and despair in equal amounts. It is final. It frustrates and saves. But it isn't forever. It must be learned and then practiced for it to be the friend you want it to be.

This is all very well and good, but it really has nothing to do with the reason you're holding this book in your hands, which is to get that little white ball in the hole more often. Maybe you've tried a hundred different ways to complete this task and are reaching out for one final dose of help, or you're a fairly accomplished putter searching for that extra edge to take your scores even lower. Either way you've come to the right place.

I've been writing golf instruction articles for the better part of 15 years, and have had the privilege of working with dozens of very talented PGA teaching professionals—including *Golf Magazine's* Top 100 Teachers—and PGA Tour pros while producing some 300 pages of instruction each year. But there's something about the book you're holding that's different. Never before have I teamed with such an elite group dedicated to a single part of the game, nor helped produce such highly researched material. The teachers that you'll learn from on the following pages are *serious*—they've dedicated their lives and careers to developing new ways and improving the old methods to help golfers sink more putts, a part of the game that—let's face it—gets second billing to driving and iron play and the big-name swing gurus so closely associated with the game's brightest stars. These putting geniuses often work in the shadows of the public spotlight, but guess whose numbers are on speed-dial when a Tour player hits a dry spell on the greens? With your purchase of this instruction manual, you now have the same level of access.

Check the roster: Mike Shannon, Dr. Craig Farnsworth, Stan Utley and Marius Filmalter—these teachers' stable of Tour students could fill both Ryder Cup sides ten times over; Maggie Will, David Edel, Mark Sweeney and Dr. David Wright—four names you may not know but soon will thanks to their ability to think outside the box and develop innovative ways to make pure contact, find the best possible putter for your game, read greens like crazy and build a perfect stance; Mike Adams and Scott Munroe—two backbone members of the Top 100 Teachers in America who constantly push the envelope to help golfers like you play better and enjoy the game more. There's enough putting brain power among this group to turn any stroke around for good.

I applaud your purchase—you recognize the importance of putting and the abilities of our all-star cast of instructors to get you on track. You're in for some serious improvement. In addition to the lessons you'll read in these pages, we've created 40-plus videos with our teachers for the ultimate learning experience. When you see the "play" icon, go to www.golf.com/bestputtingbook and click on the appropriate video. It's a great way to make sure you understand each lesson so you can take what you learn out on the course.

Armed with this book, you'll realize what all great putters have always known—putting is the difference between good scores and *winning* scores. When you start to sink putts, the rest of the game seems easy, even when you miss a fairway or an approach. Read every lesson and watch the videos—a whole new game is just a page flip or a mouse click away.

DAVID DENUNZIO
*INSTRUCTION EDITOR, GOLF MAGAZINE*

# Contributors

**THE TOUR TEACHER**

**Stan Utley**
One of the best putters of his generation. Now, he shows his former PGA Tour colleagues the right way to get it done.

**THE STROKE ANALYZER**

**Mike Adams**
The most widely published authority on the swing and stroke, and tutor to dozens of PGA Tour players and notable celebrities.

**THE MASTER FITTER**

**David Edel**
The brains behind the most complete putter-fitting system in the world can build you the perfect flatstick in minutes.

**THE BALANCE EXPERT**

**Dr. David F. Wright**
His innovative research on stance width and grip size has solved—finally—the mystery behind a perfect, balanced address.

**THE GREEN MACHINE**

**Mark Sweeney**
His AimPoint technology—the one on TV that shows how every putt tracks to the hole—is now right at your fingertips.

THE BEST PUTTING INSTRUCTION BOOK EVER!

**THE RESEARCH BRAIN**

**Marius Filmalter**
Has researched and analyzed over 50,000 pro and amateur strokes. He knows what good putters do—and what you don't do.

**THE CHANGE AGENT**

**Scott Munroe**
Top 100 Teacher is fast-becoming the go-to guy for long- and belly-putter instruction—and changing fortunes along the way.

**THE PUTT DOCTOR**

**Dr. Craig L. Farnsworth**
The most sought-after visualization coach across all sports and continents. Author of the best-seller, *See It & Sink It.*

**THE STROKE PIONEER**

**Maggie Will**
Three-time winner on the LPGA Tour and inventor of a can't-miss stroke that may well be the new way to putt.

**THE AMING EXPERT**

**Mike Shannon**
His theories on linear and nonlinear putting have made him a household name among golf's putting elite.

INSIDE

# CONTENTS

THE BEST PUTTING INSTRUCTION BOOK EVER!

**CHAPTER 1**

# How to Pick the Right Putter

**By David Edel** / The Master Fitter

Discover the head shapes, hosel, shafts and weights that allow you to produce perfect aim, path and speed.

*p. 1*

**CHAPTER 2**

# How to Build the Perfect Stance

**By Dr. David F. Wright** / The Balance Expert

The keys are stance width, grip size and a new measurement that's changing the way athletes set up in any sport.

*p. 25*

**CHAPTER 3**

# How to Calibrate Your Stroke

**By Mike Adams** / The Stroke Analyzer

How to tap your internal rhythm to stroke putts with perfect pace for expert control on any green.

*p. 41*

**CHAPTER 4**

# Mastering the Arc Stroke

**By Stan Utley** / The Tour Teacher

Learn the Tour-proven way of swinging the putter back and through with the man whose stroke could rarely be beat.

*p. 57*

**CHAPTER 5**

# Mastering the Brush Stroke

**By Maggie Will** / The Stroke Pioneer

The stroke behind three LPGA Tour wins is the most innovative in years. It's also your ticket to a smoother roll.

*p. 73*

**CHAPTER 6**

# How to Read Greens Like a Pro

**By Mark Sweeney** / The Green Machine

Take the guesswork out of green reading and replace it with a system that predicts the perfect roll every time.

*p. 93*

**CHAPTER 7**

# How to Aim at the Right Spot

**By Mike Shannon** / The Aiming Expert

Do you see putts in straight lines or do you see them in curves? The answer holds the secret to more one-putts.

*p. 111*

**CHAPTER 8**

# Golf's Best Secret: The Long Putter

**By Scott Munroe** / The Change Agent

How to tap the smooth-roll power of long and belly putters and resurrect your putting game.

*p. 127*

**CHAPTER 9**

# How to Practice for Improvement

**By Dr. Craig L. Farnsworth** / The Putt Doctor

Practice is good, but only if it's the right kind of practice. Here's how to structure your learning time for max improvement.

*p. 143*

**CHAPTER 10**

# How to Fix Your Worst Flaws

**By Marius Filmalter** / The Research Brain

Choking. Freezing. The Yips. These are more than hiccups—they're serious flaws. Here are the end-all cures.

*p. 157*

# 1

# How to Pick the Right Putter

Putting boils down to getting aim right, tracing the correct path and dialing in the right speed. There's a feel element to nailing these factors for sure, but when the putter in your hands matches the way your eyes see putts, it all comes together as if by magic.

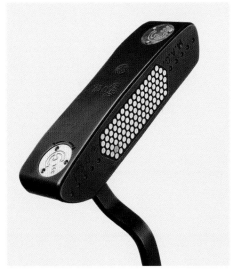

# The Master Fitter
# David Edel

*PGA teaching professional and club manufacturer, Edel Golf, Liberty Hill, Tex.*

The creator of the most advanced putter-fitting system in the world has over 300 million ways to build you the perfect putter, and he proves to you that when it comes down to solving the mysteries of putting, the arrow—not necessarily the Indian—is getting in the way.

**HY IS IT THAT** some players putt the lights out without giving their stroke anything but a passing thought, while others have to gnash their teeth to sink the simplest four-footer? It took me 14 years of researching and building putters to finally come up with a solid answer: *good putters putt with the right gear.*

I'm sure the putter that's currently in your bag is a fine flatstick, but is it absolutely the right one for you, and how would you know if it was or it wasn't? When you went to purchase it you were obviously swayed by its looks, or by the fact that your favorite Tour pro endorsed it. Either way it was a hasty decision, and not once did you ask about the head weight or grip options, nor inquire about the loft. I'm also willing to bet that you didn't carefully examine the head shape or the hosel design, or whether the putter was face-balanced or toe-weighted. These are more than just add-ons, like the sport package option on a new car. Design elements such as these are fundamental to the way any putter performs and, more important, how it reacts to your senses and stroke.

The industry wants you to believe that redemption lies at the nearest pro shop. I'll prove to you that redemption lies with *you*, and how the right combination of putter design elements can help you see the line in a whole new light—the perfect line from the ball to the hole.

**5 Things I'll Teach You In This Chapter**

**1** Why putting is an enigma—and how finding the right putter can solve it.

**2** The three components to successful putting, and how you can master them with a simple putter change.

**3** How key design elements such as hosel and head shape affect your ability to aim.

**4** How to enhance your touch and feel on the greens by changing the weight distribution in your putter.

**5** The link between your putter's design, your perception of the line and green reading.

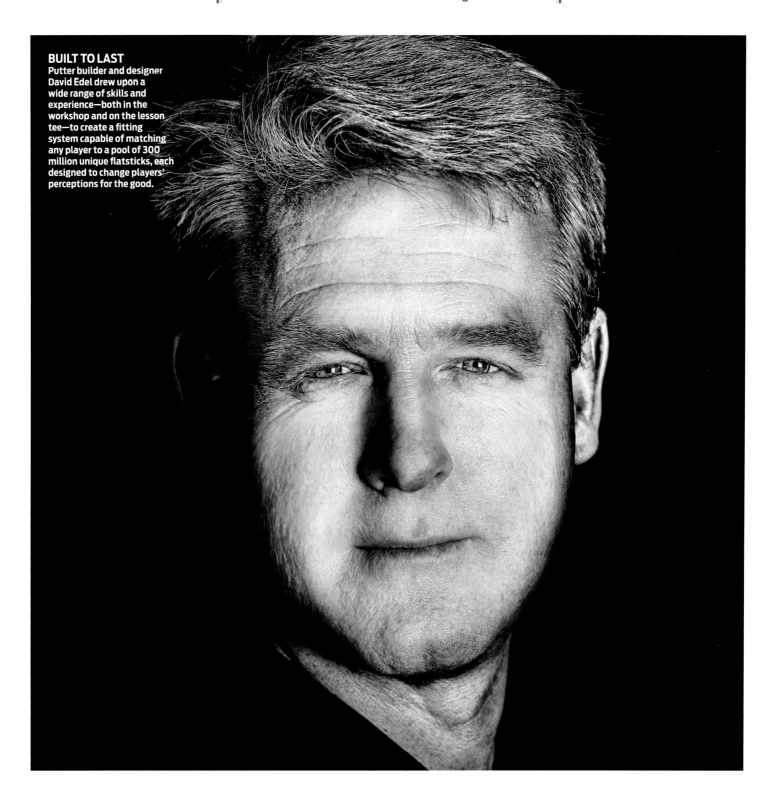

**BUILT TO LAST**
Putter builder and designer David Edel drew upon a wide range of skills and experience—both in the workshop and on the lesson tee—to create a fitting system capable of matching any player to a pool of 300 million unique flatsticks, each designed to change players' perceptions for the good.

## ALL ABOUT ME

**Name:** David Edel

**Where you can find me:** Edel Golf, Liberty Hill, Tex.

**Teaching since:** 1989

**Where I played:** Various mini-tours

**Where I've taught:** Coeur d'Alene Resort (Coeur d'Alene, Id.); Broadmoor G.C. (Portalnd, Ore.); multiple clubs in Argentina, Chile and throughout South America

**Who I've built putters for:** James Driscoll, Bo Van Pelt and 80+ other PGA Tour professionals; professional athletes Bill Russell, Bobby Orr and Sean Elliott, among others

**My best contribution to the game:** A putter-fitting process to systematically correct player aim bias, proving that the correct putter can change the way golfers putt for the better

**For more instruction:** golf.com/ bestputtingbook edelgolf.com

# "Certain head shapes, hosels, aim lines, shaft lengths and other design variables promote different patterns of aim."

**A**SK ANY OF the golfers you know—even yourself—what makes a putter a good putter, and the concept of "feel" will almost certainly be broached, although nobody can ever seem to define it. Is it how soft the grip feels, or the sound the putter makes, or its weight or loft? What about the shaft, head style, aiming lines or the hosel? Never before has a golf term been used with such frequency without anyone knowing really what it means.

My teacher, Ben Doyle, taught me early in my career that to be successful at anything you had to be able to define and sustain its core principle. He used the example of a boat: What is it? The core principle of any boat, he said, is buoyancy. That's it. If you can make it float, you've made a successful boat.

So the million-dollar question: What's the core principle of feel? My studies show that it's a combination of three factors: aim, path and speed control. Every decision you make on every putt is based on these three factors, and they're tightly interrelated—if you try something different in your aim you're going to get something new with your speed and path. That's why I call it the Putting Triad. For example, let's say you typically aim left of your target (many people do). Over the years you've learned to compensate for your left-aim bias by opening the putterface or cutting across the ball at impact. Then you suddenly learn how to aim straight. Good for you, but now your path and speed don't match your aim. You're going to miss right if you don't change the other parts of the Triad.

The most important thing to know about the Putting Triad—and to fully grasp the core principle of putting and feel—is that it's dominated by aim. Aim is step one to becoming a great putter. It's the reason why you stroke putts a certain way (like in the left-aim bias example above). Your mind senses where you aim and makes the necessary adjustments.

A lot of what you're going to read in this book deals with improving your aim, but that won't mean a thing unless you have a putter that allows you to do it. I began making putters 14 years ago for Henry Griffitts, and I also helped them develop their fitting system. During the process we discovered that the physical makeup of a putter created aim bias. In other words, certain head shapes, hosels, aim lines, shaft lengths and other design variables promoted different patterns of aim—left, straight and right. Once we understood that, we decided to build a system to test and evaluate different combinations of components to create consistent aim patterns in individual players. I've recently adapted these principles to my own company, Edel Golf, where we have the ability to build 16 million different putters with various component combinations to enhance aim and performance. While it may be hard for you to believe that a few extra grams of head weight or a hosel swap are the difference between a make and a miss, it's nonetheless true—a fact that you'll come to accept as you learn more about the different components and their effects on the Triad.

## THE PUTTING TRIAD

1. Consists of aim, path and speed control.
2. Aim is the dominant member of the Triad, and you can aim correctly only if the putter in your hands features design variables that allow you to.

## WATCH & LEARN

 When you see this icon, go to **golf.com/ bestputtingbook** for a free video lesson with David Edel.

**AIM OF THE GAME**
Putting success is determined by your aim, path and speed. The most important of these is aim, which you can master only if you have the right putter.

# AIM IS KING

**DESPITE THE GLUT** of putting instruction articles and training aids that deal with stroke path and acceleration, the direction your putts travel is primarily determined by the putterface and where it's pointed. That's an easy enough concept to get one's head around—the ball goes where the face goes. But there's more to aim than pointing the face left, right or center. Aim is also a vertical concept. Not only do you have to aim the putter in the right direction laterally, but also up and down.

## GAUGE YOUR PERSPECTIVE

If you have the chance, set up to putt to a mark on a wall about three-quarters of an inch above the floor. Make it from 12 feet or so. Then have a friend attach a laser to your putterface (you can pick one up at any pro shop) and see where it points. A wide majority of golfers will not only miss the mark to the left or the right, but also above and below. They miss in two dimensions. They miss laterally because they're pointing the face left or right of where they think they're aiming, and above and below because a) they're not aware of the exact amount of loft in the putterface, or b) they set their hands ahead or behind the putterface, which tilts the entire head up and down.

Nearly everyone fails this test because most golfers don't give any thought to the various design elements built into their putter and how these elements affect aim. Putters aren't just putters. They're a conglomeration of complex shapes, curves and angles—visuals that your eyes have to sort out in order to point everything in the right direction. Your eyes can't do it if any of these shapes don't look good to

> "Not only do you have to aim the putter in the right direction laterally, but also up and down."

**PUTTER PRINCIPLE**
Your ability to aim your putter in the direction you intend is heavily influenced by the design components in your putter. The fact is that some putters definitely allow you to aim better than others.

you or inhibit your perspective. Since golfers aren't fully aware of this fact (evidenced by the fact that 90 percent of the players I test can't aim straight on a six-foot putt), they make compensations in their strokes—again, altering each segment of the Triad in a desperate attempt to get the ball in the hole.

## CUSTOMIZING YOUR PERSPECTIVE

The laser test mentioned above is the first step of my fitting process. The test I use is a bit more sophisticated, but the same principle applies *[see panel, right]*. Once I know a player's aim bias (up and left, down and right, etc.) I start manipulating the angles, lines and curves in their putter until they match their eye. I do this with a proprietary system that allows me to change 10 key putter-design variables with what amounts to a simple turn of an Allen wrench. Each one of these variables affects your perception of where you're aiming the putterface. It sounds crazy, but it's true—a putterhead with two aiming lines will cause you to aim differently than one with three, and an S-shaped hosel gives you a totally different perspective than an L-shaped hosel. These aren't new discoveries—we've known about them for the better part of 14 years. I'm sure you've heard the story about bad habits and them being hard to break.

While there are many design variables that go into every putter and that affect your visual aim, we'll cover the primary pieces in this chapter to give you a solid understanding of how each and every one changes your perspective and each component of the Triad. Armed with this knowledge, you'll be well on your way to making much more informed purchasing decisions and aiming your putter where you've always wanted to: right at your target.

| AIM MODIFIERS | SPEED MODIFIERS |
|---|---|
| HOSEL | LOFT |
| LIE ANGLE | HEAD WEIGHT |
| HEAD SHAPE | COUNTER WT. |
| LOFT | SHAFT FLEX |
| LINES | |
| LENGTH | |
| GRIP TYPE | |

**AIM TEST**
Aiming is a multidimensional concept: there's a left/right component and an up/down component. I assess a player's aim by reflecting a laser beam off a mirror that I attach to the player's putterface. This allows me to pinpoint both the vertical and horizontal aim tendencies. Nearly everyone mis-aims in both dimensions, but they can improve aim by swapping putter components that confuse their eyes for ones that look good to them.

**STEP 2**
Once the student is comfortable with his aim, I remove the ball. In most cases, the rebound of the laser off the mirror misses the target to the left or right as well above or below (a backboard behind the laser shows exactly where the putterface is aimed).

**STEP 1**
I point a laser beam at a ball and have the student aim the putterface back at the laser. With perfect aim, the mirror on the putterface should reflect the laser back to its origin.

# AIM MODIFIER #1: THE HOSEL

**THERE ARE A** number of putter models where the shaft dives straight into the head, but most of the putters you'll see on the market feature a distinct hosel—that funny-shaped connecting piece between the end of the shaft and the putterhead. Hosel type has a lot to do with the overall balance of your putter. Certain shapes create face balancing and varying degrees of toe hang—design traits that are easy to pick up (just balance a putter on your index finger slightly above the hosel to see how it's weighted). What isn't so concrete is the effect that different hosel types have on your perspective and aim. As it is with all of the putter-design variables that we'll discuss in this chapter, the shape of the hosel has a definite influence on your ability to point the putterface in the direction you intend.

The easiest way to survey any hosel is to break it down by shape (usually S-shaped or L-shaped) and by offset (usually 0 to 0.5 inches). Hosel offset and shape produce optical geometries that create aim responses in your subconscious. Some tend to aim you more to the left and some tend to aim you more to the right. The critical word here is "more"—a certain hosel may aim you more right or more left, but not necessarily right or left of dead center. The hosel is the only putter component that we'll discuss that doesn't seal the deal in and of itself. Also notice that I used the word "tend" because everyone is wired differently.

That being said, here are some general rules that hold true for the majority of players:

**1. L-SHAPED HOSELS** (also known as plumber-necks) tend to create more of a leftward aim bias than their S-shaped counterparts.

**2. HOSELS THAT FEATURE OFFSET** tend to aim players more to the left. It's a progressive relationship; the greater the offset, the greater the left-aim bias.

**3. ONSET HOSELS** (those that set the putter-face ahead of the shaft) tend to aim people more to the right.

**S-SHAPED HOSEL**

**PICK YOUR HOSEL**
Check the hosel designs on these pages (as well as the view you get with each one when you stand over the ball). Even though these are simple photographic representations, you should be able to sense how your perspective changes with each one. My fitting system uses five S-shaped hosels and six L-shaped hosels (I machine an L-shaped hosel with a forward shaft insert that isn't pictured here) with varying offset to create 11 unique views at address.

**L-SHAPED HOSEL**

**NOTE** If a person uses a putter with a lot of offset but tends to aim right, giving him a putter with zero offset will most likely change his aim bias to the left. Like I mentioned previously, every player is wired differently. We never know how a player will respond until we test them using the laser and take a full inventory of their current putter preferences.

## S-SHAPED HOSELS (slant necks)

Offset created with curved rather than straight angles. As the offset increases, so does the tendency to aim more to the left.

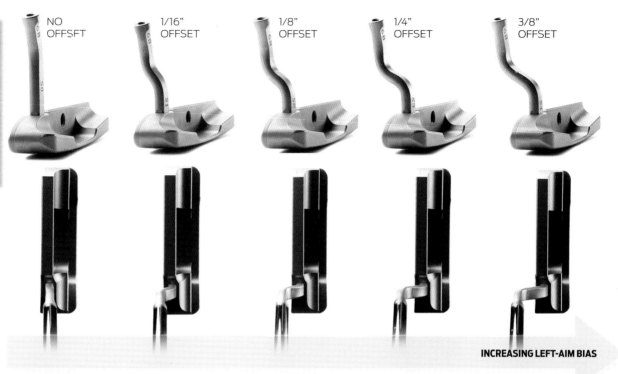

NO OFFSET    1/16" OFFSET    1/8" OFFSET    1/4" OFFSET    3/8" OFFSET

INCREASING LEFT-AIM BIAS

## L-SHAPED HOSELS (plumber necks)

Offset created with the addition of a 90-degree bend in the hosel. Because of the straight lines designed into these hosels, L-shaped necks tend to aim players more to the left.

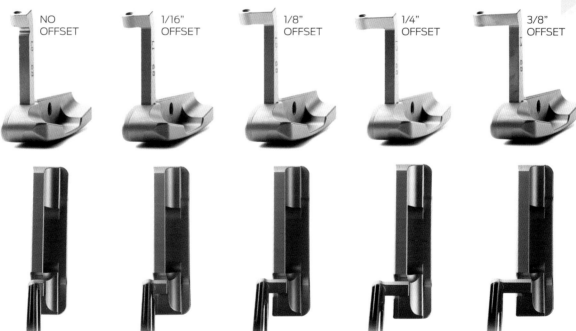

NO OFFSET    1/16" OFFSET    1/8" OFFSET    1/4" OFFSET    3/8" OFFSET

# AIM MODIFIER #2: LIE ANGLE

**LIKE YOUR IRONS,** wedges and woods, your putter is built with a specific lie—the angle that the shaft makes as it enters the hosel measured from the ground. Most off-the-rack putters are built with a minum of 71 degrees of lie.

Lie angle has a lot to do with putter aim—the manner in which it combines with the loft of your putterface and the overall length of the shaft can drastically alter your perspective. The best example to help explain how lie affects aim is when the putter is too upright. Most players compensate for too much lie by simply dropping their hands, a move that causes the toe of the putter to rise off the ground. I'm sure you know of someone who putts this way. This toe-up position almost always forces players to aim more to the left. It's the same phenomenon as setting up to the ball on a sidehill lie with the ball above your feet. The ground, lie angle and loft automatically change the clubface position and point it to the left. That's why you're told to aim out to the right on these shots because they naturally want to fly to the left.

**LIE BIAS**
As the lie angle becomes more upright *[rear putter]* the left-aim bias increases.

**LIE ANGLE**
Defined as the angle the shaft makes with the ground. Upright lies tend to aim you more to the left; flat lies tend to aim you more to the right.

**"The manner in which lie combines with loft and shaft length can drastically alter your perspective."**

# AIM MODIFIER #3: HEAD SHAPE

**IF YOU WALK** into any pro shop there's a good chance that the shear number of head designs will overwhelm you. You'd think that there were at least as many head designs as there are golfers. But when it comes down to looking at head shapes and their affect on aim and the other factors in the Triad, you can easily pare down the offerings into just a few discernable shapes.

At one end of the spectrum are large, mallet-shaped putters, like the popular Odyssey 2-Ball putters. At the other end are your standard heel-toe putters, like the PING Anser. Every other putter is a deviation of these two models. The primary difference between the two ends of the spectrum, other than size, is the geometry in the back. Mallets tend to have curved trailing edges; blades and Anser-style putters tend to feature straight back edges with a lot of parallel lines built into the head. The back geometry of any head shape is the secret to its effect on aim. Here are some general rules:

**1.** The more circular the putter's trailing edge, the more likely it will cause you to aim more to the right.

**2.** The straighter the putter's trailing edge, the more likely it will cause you to aim more to the left.

Much of this aim bias is based on where a putter forces you to look when you're setting up at address. Because a mallet features a circular back, you have to look to the leading edge to set the face perpendicular to your target line. With an Anser-style putter you can use either the back edge or the lead edge, since both are parallel.

## SHAPE SHIFTS
When surveying any putterhead, look to the back edge. The greater the curve built into the trailing edge, the more likely the putter will cause you to aim more to the right.

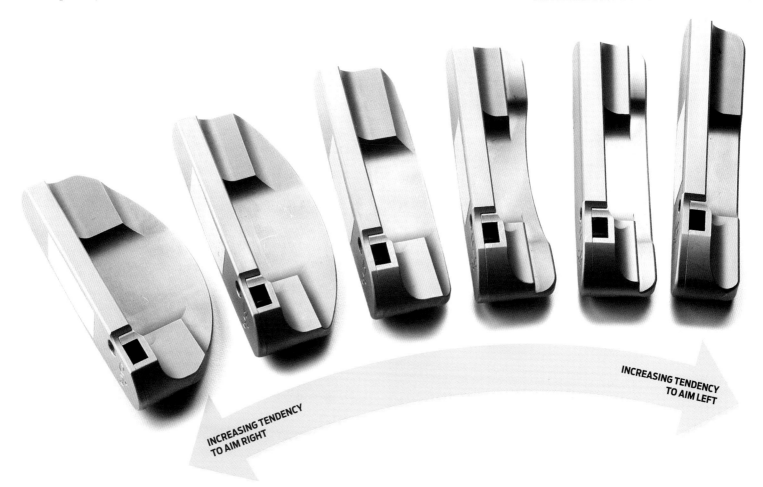

INCREASING TENDENCY TO AIM RIGHT

INCREASING TENDENCY TO AIM LEFT

# AIM MODIFIER #4: LOFT

**TRUE OR FALSE:** When you bought the putter that's currently in your bag, you paid zero attention to how much loft was built into the putterface. I'm guessing "true." It could have 3 degrees of loft or it could have 6—you have no idea. The problem here is that too little or too much loft, as it's perceived by your mind's eye—causes a double-whammy in error because it directly and dramatically affects your aim *and* your speed.

## THE EFFECT OF LOFT ON AIM

The manner in which loft affects aim has a lot to do with how you perceive the putter at address. Putters with too much loft naturally appear hooked to most players, and those with too little loft look open. There are two commonly used methods to offset the perceived look. One is to adjust aim: aim more to the right if the putter looks hooked and more to the left if the putter looks open. The other is to adjust hand position. If, for example, the putter features too much loft and appears hooked at address, you can forward-press your hands to correct the perceived face angle. However, this move also changes the loft (forward-pressing reduces the effective loft of the putterface) and shifts the point around which the putter rotates during your stroke. Imagine the compensations you now must make in your motion to offset this glut of changes. Wouldn't it be better to simply buy a putter with less loft?

**NOTE:** The effective loft of any putter is tightly related to the hosel design. In general, hosels with less offset require more loft, while hosels built with significant offset require less. This has to do with the shaft angle at address and impact relative to where the hosel positions the head.

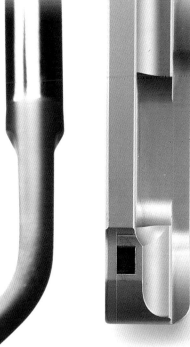

**DOUBLE DUTY**
Loft is the only putter design variable that directly affects both loft and speed.

**OPEN LOOK**
The more loft decreases, the more open the face looks at address.

**HOOKED LOOK**
As loft increases, so does your perception that the face is hooked (pointing to the left).

## A SECONDARY EFFECT: SPEED

Loft also influences the speed of your putts. The base effect is easy to understand: a ball struck with a putter built with 1 degree of loft will travel farther than one struck with a putter featuring 5 degrees of loft with the same stroke. The more important effect is a little tougher to grasp, and has to do with effective loft (the true loft of the club plus the angle at which the putter ascends into the ball). As your putter approaches impact your mind is subconsciously calculating effective loft. If it senses that your putterface has too much or too little loft based on the roll distance it computed when you made your read, it starts making adjustments. Since your mind can't magically alter the shape of your putterhead, it manipulates your stroke to change the ascent angle and get the effective loft it thinks the putt needs. This, obviously, is a slippery slope.

# AIM MODIFIER #5: LINES

**THE LINES DRAWN** on your putterhead are also critical to the aim scenario. Most people assume that you need to have lines on the putter, and that lines ensure that you'll aim straight. We see them on airstrips, highways, railway lines and race tracks, and it makes sense that we think that they're helpful. However, lines can exert both positive and negative effects depending on how your eyes interpret them. Not only is it a question of whether or not to have aim lines, but also where they should be placed and how many should be used.

We created a line template as part of our fitting system that allows us to easily test line arrangements and gauge aiming ability. The results are incredible. Here's a quick recap:

1. **Lines, in general aim, tend to make people aim left.**
2. **The farther back the lines are, the more they'll tend to aim you left.**
3. **Lines near the topline influence aim less than those placed nearer the bottom cavity.**
4. **An absence of lines tends to create a right aim bias.**

The reason for theses biases is that lines and the way they're patterned affect which part of the putter you look at. If there are more lines on the back cavity than on the leading edge, you're more likely to look at the back cavity. If there are more lines on the topline than then the back cavity, your attention will be drawn to the front of the putter, changing your perspective of the hosel, the putterhead—everything. Most people are drawn to things that look busier on a conscious level because they assume that those markings are there for a beneficial reason, but on a subconscious level they can confuse your mind sees them as just another series of inputs it needs to sort out.

**LINE STUDY**
Look for more than just colored lines. The inherent shape of your putter is a form of aiming line, as are milled notches and cutaways.

**NOTES ON COLOR**
Our line study also proved that the color of the lines affects players' aim. A gray putter with a black line and a black putter with a white line create different aim values, all other things being equal. A white line on a black putter is more evident than a black line on a gray putter. Green and red lines affect aim differently than those that are blue or yellow. Colors mean a lot to people, and they can have negative, positive, and neutral associations with them, so it would make sense that they would affect how people value them.

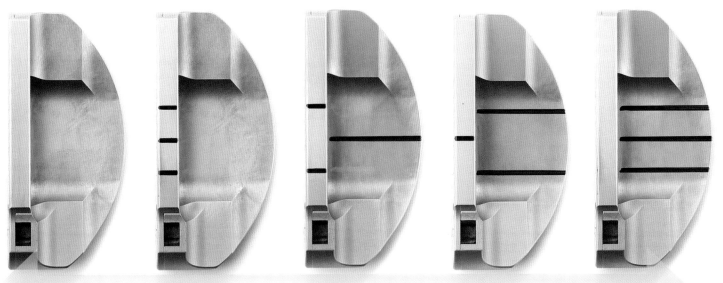

INCREASING RIGHT-AIM BIAS

INCREASING LEFT-AIM BIAS

# SPEED MODIFERS

**SO FAR YOU'VE** learned how different putter design components can affect your ability to point your putter correctly at your target. (There are a few other components that affect aim that we didn't discuss, namely shaft length, shaft flex, grip type and grip size. If you're interested in learning more about these components, visit www.edelgolf.com.) But what about the other elements of the Triad? As you can guess, the physical makeup of your putter also influences your speed and path.

Without getting into the techniques and concepts of how to produce better speed, I'll show you how putter-design variables affect your ability to control it. As with most of the concepts discussed thus far, this isn't a one-sided affair. When I talk about speed control I'm really dealing with several variables that change your sense of touch and feel.

### THE NOTION OF SCALES
Have you ever thought of your hands as pressure scales? Probably not, but if you think about it, it makes sense. Our hands can sense hot and cold, smooth and rough. They can also sense weight.

When you grab something, you don't immediately grab it with maximum force. You use just enough effort to lift it. If your hands then sense that the object is heavy, they'll increase the pressure. If your hands sense that the object is very heavy, then your body starts a complex reaction to ready and activate other muscles in your arms and torso—your legs if need be—to complete the task. All this happens, however, in relation to the sensory input provided by your hands when they first lift the object. Over time you program how much effort you need to lift certain objects, which is why you never have to think too much about the amount of energy you need to lift most items.

When you putt, the same scenario applies—your fingers and hands are the primary source for information transfer. As you make your putting stroke, the stresses of the motion create load patterns in your hands. The load patterns inform your hands if the motion is too

quick or too slow and, in nanoseconds, your body adjusts (i.e., hits the brakes or steps on the gas). This is about as close to an explanation of "feel" as you're ever going to get—a biomechanical sense of load and pressure. Over the years you've programmed the energy you need to hit putts of certain lengths (just like you learned how much pressure to use to lift everyday items), but as you're about to discover this program rarely works because the conditions affecting your putt, namely green speed, are constantly changing.

> ## "There are ways to manipulate the weight of your putter to generate the same feel and control speed on any type of green."

### HOW WEIGHT CONTROLS SPEED
Now that you know your hands receive pressure, and your brain computes a value to this pressure for a given activity, you can start to move forward with the idea that the physical makeup of your putter can affect your ability to control the speed of your putts.

Let's assume that you're a golfer who typically plays on greens that roll around 9 on the Stimpmeter (a solid average on most of the courses you'll play). Today, however, you're playing on greens that roll 11. You can guess what happens. You send your first few putts screaming past the hole, then get tentative and start coming up way short. By the time you reach the seventh hole you haven't come close to sinking a putt, the psychological bombs are detonating in your head and you haven't a clue what to do.

This is where weight comes into play, and the reason for all this talk of scales. Golfers have difficulty controlling the speed of their putts because they haven't learned to outsmart their feel senses to get what they want. In other words, there are ways to manipulate the weight component of your putter to generate the same feel and control speed on any type of green—fast, slow, whatever. The trick is to make your hands sense more weight or less weight than they expect so they relay new information to your brain, which then tells your body to move the putter faster or slower than what you have already programmed. Voila!—instant speed control.

Here's an easy way to understand how the system works. Pick a spot 10 feet in front of you. Imagine tossing a Ping-Pong ball to that spot. Now, toss a bowling ball with the same force you used with the Ping-Pong ball. The bowling ball travels less, not because of a change in force or velocity, but because of a change in weight.

This explains why, if you're old enough to remember, pros used to add or remove lead tape from their putters before play. If they didn't have enough practice time to adjust their previously programmed strokes to the pace of that day's greens, they'd make their putter heavier or lighter to force their hands to adjust for them.

### ALTERING WEIGHT FOR YOUR GOOD
Manipulating weight is the fast track to nailing the speed part of the Putting Triad. There's more to it, however, than simply beefing up the gram weight in the head. Weighting covers a variety of putter-design properties, including counterweighting (adding weight to the grip end of the shaft) and, believe it or not, shaft flex. It's important to fine-tune these variables so that they can work with your natural touch system. Trust me—there's a system to dialing in these components. Once you become familiar with the system on the following pages, you'll see that the problems you've had controlling the speed and distance you hit your putts haven't been your fault at all.

**SPEED CONTROL**
If you have difficulty controlling how far you hit your putts, then you're in need of a head-weight change or a different shaft flex.

# SPEED MODIFIER #1: HEAD WEIGHT

**HEAD WEIGHT IS** exactly what you think it is—how much does that puppy weigh? The best overall head weight for you is the one that matches the speed of the majority of greens you play (i.e., those at your home course or your most frequently played muni). If, however, you tend to play a number of different courses, then your best putter is one that allows you to easily add weight or remove it, since you're going to experience several different green speeds over the course of a year and you'll need the ability to adjust. (Keep in mind that as the seasons change, so do the conditions of the greens, so even if you play the same course over and over you may benefit from an adjustable-weight putter).

As a rule, you should use a lighter-weight putter on slow greens and a heavier-weight putter on fast greens. I know it makes sense that you'd do just the opposite, since a heavier putter transfers more energy to the ball than a lighter one with the same stroke, and that's the last thing you want on fast greens. It doesn't work that way, however. Your hands sense that the putter is heavy and, therefore, will swing it with less effort.

If you remember your high school physics, you'll recall the formula $E=MV^2$. It's the equation for Energy, which is equal to the Mass of the object multiplied by the square of its Velocity. Regardless of the grade you received in physics, it's easy to see just by looking at the formula that velocity has a much greater influence on energy than mass.

## GETTING THE WEIGHT RIGHT

So how do you figure out how to get the weight right in your putterhead? Simple—tack a piece of string on the putting green, set up 10 feet away from it on level ground and roll a few putts toward it *[photo, right]*. If you hit most of the putts long and short of the string, then you know that you lack the touch to control distance with the weight built into your putter. I guarantee that if you change the weight,

**WEIGHT WATCHER**
The addition or removal of weight from the head is key to dialing in the correct speed on the greens you typically play.

you'll fine-tune your distance control and hit the string every time. If you hit most of your putts beyond the string, your putter is too light. You're moving it too fast because your hands sense the lack of weight. If the majority of your putts stop short of the string, then your putter is too heavy. You're moving it too slow;y because your hands sense too much weight. Remember, velocity has a greater effect on energy than mass.

Of course, some golfers hit putts farther with a heavy putter and some hit putts shorter with a lighter putter, but not because of the weight. When you putt with a putter that's too heavy for your senses, it starts off moving at a slower pace, as discussed. What can and very often happens is that your brain picks up on the movement and sends the message to accelerate. The acceleration, however, happens too quickly, too late and at too rapid a pace—you jab at the ball (can you say "yips?"). The opposite can and often happens when you swing a putter that's too light. This time, once your brain senses that the putter is moving too fast (because your hands sense the lighter weight), it dumps the power and you decelerate—a very common and serious error.

The key is to experiment with the string drill using putters of various weight (I'm sure your local pro shop has a row of differently weighted putters and a practice putting mat—take advantage of it). My fitting system allows me to change the weight in the head up to 64 grams in a matter of seconds. It's an important part of the Edel Golf system. Usually we can nail distance control in just a few strokes.

> "As a general rule, you should use a lighter-weight putter on slow greens and a heavier-weight putter on fast greens."

**SELF TEST**
Rolling balls to a string tells you a lot about the consistency of your stroke and the putter components you need to change to get the right speed and direction every time.

# SPEED MODIFIER #2: SHAFT FLEX

**THE SHAFT ON** your putter does more than connect the grip to the putterhead. Its length is a key component to nailing your aim (we'll save that for another time) and its flex is an important speed determinant. Flex is closely tied to the weight of your putterhead and the manner in which you accelerate as you make your stroke. Softer flexes make the head feel heavier and stiff flexes make the shaft feel lighter. Here's an example. I had a customer who returned his putter because he wanted me to add more weight to the putterhead. From his file I knew that the current head weight was absolutely perfect for him, so instead of altering that spec I simply put a softer shaft in. The customer rang after a few days to ask me how much weight I added to the putter because he was rolling the ball perfectly!

You can discover the best flex for you the same way you discover the appropriate head weight. Go back to rolling balls to a string and experiment with different shaft flexes until you can consistently hit the distance on the money. Changing the flex is the same as changing the weight—softening the shaft makes the putterhead feel heavier, and stiffening the shaft makes the head feel lighter. (The opposite also holds true: adding weight makes the shaft feel softer, and removing weight from the head makes the shaft feel stiffer).

## ACCELERATION EFFECTS

The weight/flex relationship isn't the only one that affects speed. The relative softness or stiffness you feel in the shaft has a lot to do with the way you accelerate the putter as you make your stroke. The faster you accelerate, the more the shaft will flex. Less acceleration makes the shaft feel stiffer.

*There are two ways you can accelerate:*

**1. Radial Acceleration:** A motion originating from the center and working outward, like swinging a rock tied to a string. This is the acceleration found in arc strokes (see Chapter 4).

**2. Linear Acceleration:** A motion originating from a thrust that's parallel to the ground, like the back-and-forth motion of a piston. This is the acceleration used in most pendulum strokes and in Maggie Will's Brush Stroke (Chapter 5).

Most golfers prefer to accelerate one way or another, which may help explain why certain golfers prefer to swing their putter on an arc (radial accelerators) or straight back and through (linear accelerators). Problems

happen when you mix and match. In other words, you either look like Jack Nicklaus, a linear putter, or Tiger Woods, a radial putter, or you look frustrated because you try to look like both.

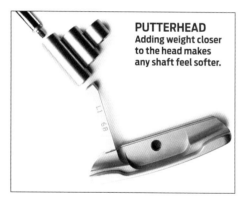

**PUTTERHEAD**
Adding weight closer to the head makes any shaft feel softer.

**CUSTOMIZE**
Manipulating weight in three key areas of your putter *[circled]* changes the way the shaft flexes and the speed at which you roll putts.

---

**YOU KNOW YOU'RE A RADIAL ACCELERATOR IF:**
● You tend to make long strokes and accelerate the putter gradually.
● You like to adjust for putt distance by varying the length of your stroke, not the force of it.
● Your backstroke is usually longer than your forward-stroke.
● You're good at speed putts and lags.

**EQUIPMENT PRESCRIPTION:**
Go for heavier head weights and softer shaft flexes.

---

**YOU KNOW YOU'RE A LINEAR ACCELERATOR IF:**
● You tend to keep your stroke length the same and add or remove thrust to control the distance you hit your putts.
● You prefer a short backstroke and an accelerating through-stroke
● You're okay on short putts but longer putts give you fits.

**EQUIPMENT PRESCRIPTION:**
Opt for stiffer shafts and extra weight either in the middle of the shaft or at the grip (counterweight).

# SPEED MODIFIER #3: COUNTERWEIGHT

**HAVE YOU EVER** changed your putter grip? A lot of golfers do to create a new look or feel in their flatstick, or to adjust to their hand size. While these types of changes are always made with good intentions, they seriously alter the overall performance of your putter. Standard grips can vary in weight by as much as 30 to 40 grams even though they look and feel similar. Gripping your putter with a midsize or jumbo grip can add up to 110 extra grams. What golfers don't realize is that adding weight to the handle makes the head feel lighter, which you've already learned has drastic implications when it comes to speed control.

Manipulating weight at the grip end of the putter, also known as counterweighting, is a relatively new concept in putters. In the grip example above the counterweight was used as a negative. Under the watchful eye of a fitter, however, adding weight to the handle—and sometimes the middle of the shaft—is an effective way to improve the way the putter reacts in your hands. Our fitting system is replete with multiple ways to alter the weight of the grip end and the shaft to not only match the speed-control needs of individual players, but

also their aim. Here's how it works:

### IF YOU TEND TO AIM MORE TO THE LEFT...
● **Experiment with counterweights either in the handle or the shaft.** My research shows that counterweights promote a sense of blocking, which helps left aimers compensate for their bias. Also, left aimers tend to be more linear in their acceleration patterns, and the extra handle weight gives them something to push against. (Once a left-aim bias is corrected, however, counterweights are no longer effective for these individuals.)

### IF YOU TEND TO AIM MORE TO THE RIGHT...
● **Avoid counterweights and experiment with different head weights,** since the extra handle or shaft weight promotes a sense that you're blocking the putt—a double whammy. Once you correct your right aim, however, counterweights can be of great service. Most right aimers tend to retain the outside-in stroke they used to compensate for right aim even after they learn how to aim straight. Counterweighting relaxes this outside-in motion since it's more difficult to release the putterhead with extra weight toward the handle.

### HOW MUCH COUNTERWEIGHTING, IF ANY, IS RIGHT FOR YOU?
Again, the string test holds the key. Also, since counterweighting affects aim as well as speed, you should putt balls to a specific target to gauge how the weights affect your direction (left or right) as well as your distance. You can easily add weight to the handle or shaft with simple lead tape (available in any pro shop).

> "Adding weight to the handle makes the head feel lighter, which has drastic implications when it comes to speed control."

**SHAFT**
Weighted shaft inserts can enhance the feel of a straight-back-and-through stroke.

**GRIP**
Counterweighting is a powerful tool to improve the shape and feel of your stroke.

# COMPLETING THE TRIAD: PATH

**WE'VE TALKED A** lot about aim and speed, but what about the third member of the Triad, path? There's not much you can do to your putter to affect path compared to aim and speed, but it's important to know that the path of your stroke is entirely dependent on where you aim and at what speed you hit the putt, two components of the Triad that can definitely be affected by changing your putter. So in a sense, the physical makeup of your putter has a lot to say about how you swing it back and through.

## DEALING IN QUADRANTS

The best way to see how your putter makeup and the Triad work together is to recognize that every putt you'll ever face starts in one of four quadrants surrounding the hole. Basically, there are four sides to every cup situated around what's called a Zero Line, which is the line on which the ball rolls without any curve (you'll learn all about this with green-reading pioneer Mark Sweeney in Chapter 6). Check the photo at left to see how the quadrant works, and pay attention to how mistakes in your aim affect your path and speed.

---

Quadrant 1: Downhill right-to-left putt.
Quadrant 2: Uphill right-to-left putt.
Quadrant 3: Uphill left-to-right putt.
Quadrant 4: Downhill left-to-right putt.

---

**When Your Putt is in Quadrant 1**, the true aim point is right of the hole. If you have a right-aim bias, you'll miss the putt wide right unless you alter your path by pulling the ball or hit the ball with less speed. If you have a left-aim bias, you'll miss the putt on the left unless you alter your path by pushing the ball or adding speed to remove some of the break.

**When Your Putt is in Quadrant 2**, the true aim point, again, is right of the hole. If you have a right-aim bias, you'll miss the putt wide right unless you alter your path by pulling the ball or hiting the ball with less speed. If you have

a left-aim bias, you'll miss the putt on the left unless you alter your path by pushing the ball or adding speed to remove some of the break. There's the additional problem in that this putt, as with the putt in Quadrant 3, is uphill, and every golfer has a built-in tendency to hit this putt harder to track the right line.

**When Your Putt is in Quadrant 3**, the true aim point is left of the hole. If you're a left aimer you're already pointing your putterface above the true aim point, so there's no help in hitting the ball harder as you subconsciously do on uphill putts—you'll just miss to the left quicker. A speed adjustment may help a right aimer, since it will offset the fact that they're set up to play less break.

**When Your Putt is in Quadrant 4**, the left aimer is already aimed above the true aim point (left of the hole), but since this putt is downhill, changing the path by pushing the ball is a scary proposition because of the speed. Similar trouble awaits a right-aimer—any additional speed here or a change in path will make for a scary second putt if the first one misses.

In conclusion, path always changes to meet the requirements of speed and aim, and as the four quadrants show, altering path—as well as speed—to compensate for aim makes things very difficult. Use your equipment to fine tune your aim and speed and your path will almost always correct itself on its own, making holing putts from each of the quadrants a matter of simply making a good read and then smoothly pulling the trigger.

> "Path always changes to meet the requirements of speed and aim, and altering path to compensate for aim makes things very difficult."

---

**QUAD PUTTING**
This chart shows you the difference between the true aim and the expected path for each putt in all four sections of the quad. If your bias—or putter—forces you to aim left or right of the true aim point, you'll have to adjust by manipulating speed and the path of your stroke. This is difficult to pull off with consistent results, mandating the need to get aim right in the first place with a putter that allows you to.

# BUILDING THE PERFECT PUTTER

**I HOPE THAT** this information has helped you realize the value of playing with the correct putter. Within this realization lies the platform to develop a competent putting game. The complexities built into this aspect of the game are many, so taking a nonsensical approach can be dangerous. That's the real value I see in my fitting system: there's a concrete, justifiable reason behind every hosel change and additional gram added to the putterhead. Each alteration is made with the same goal in mind: improving all of the factors in your Putting Triad. As I mentioned previously, I can build 300 million unique putters with the components stocked in my fitting cart *[photo, oppposite page].* With the right knowledge, you can weed out the ones that won't work for you based on your tendencies and find one that helps you putt the lights out.

My views on putter-fitting and enhancing the Triad are not mine alone. I would like to thank my friend Mike Schy, a great teacher and professional, for listening to my theories and providing positive feedback; David Orr, Director of Instruction at Campbell University PGM Program, for contributing to my knowledge and testing ideas to validate the value of putter-fitting; my partner and head

machinist, Cliff Dorsey, made my ideas a reality and, in my opinion, works of art; Bobby Dean, for selling enough putters to keep us alive; Mark Sweeney, for giving us his knowledge about green reading (Chapter 6) and creating the final major piece to the puzzle;

Geoff Mangum, for tenaciously studying the putting game and sharing his information; and teaching legend Chuck Cook, my first account, who gave me the credibility to reach out and expand this exciting new world of putter-fitting to outlets nationwide.

## THE PERFECT PUTTER IN 20 SECONDS

**LOFT**
I have specially designed face plates with 0 to 5 degrees of loft that attach and un-attach easily to the head.

**TURN STYLE**
I can change 10 different head and shaft components with a special tool of my own design in an instant.

**HOSEL**
A choice of 11 hosel styles makes it easy to fit a student for his aim bias after I asses his aiming tendencies with the laser.

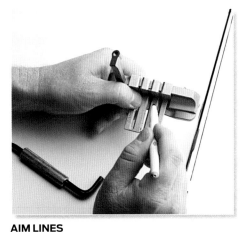

**AIM LINES**
Another of my inventions is a stencil that allows me to experiment with multiple aim lines and arrangements when dialing in a student's aim.

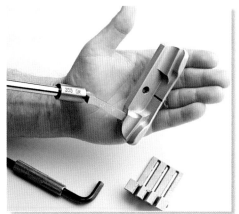

**READY TO GO**
Once all the pieces are in place, the specs for the fitting are noted and built into hand-milled putters machined at my shop near Austin, Tex.

**FIT FOR SCORING**
My fitting system allows me to match golfers with a putter that impoves aim, speed and path in a matter of minutes.

# 2

# How to Build the Perfect Stance

Address is the most overlooked part of putting. Even the players who work at it do so without thinking about the three most critical areas: stance width, grip size and a new measurement called the Angle of Symmetry. These are not simple basics—they're the secrets to consistently holing putts.

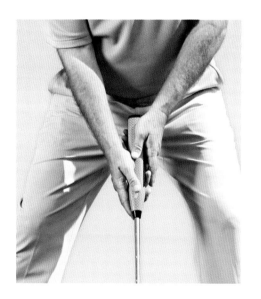

# The Balance Expert
# David Wright

*GOLF Magazine Top 100 Teacher, Wright Balance Golf Schools, Mission Viejo, Calif.*

My research on stance width and grip size proves you can't address a putt in balance without nailing these two setup elements. I'll show you how to get them right with a unique whole-body measuring technique that's changing the way athletes approach any contact sport.

**A**LTHOUGH I'VE BEEN teaching golf for close to 30 years, I've dedicated a lot of my time to studying the psychology of learning and how the mind and body work together to perform motor skills. These interests led me to a three-year research project in Dr. Frank Jobe's Biomechanics Lab at Centinela Hospital in Los Angeles in 2004. During this time I studied the way golfers typically distribute weight across their feet, and how their ability to balance—or lack thereof—affected their full swings and putting strokes. We analyzed hundreds of golfers and collected massive amounts of data in search of a balance silver bullet. In the end, we found three.

The most significant of these discoveries is what I call the Angle of Symmetry, an angle that your body tends to create over and over (in your back, knees, arms, etc.) when you execute a motor skill in perfect balance. Everyone has an Angle of Symmetry, and the more you incorporate it in your setup and stroke the better your results will be—as in "off-the-charts" better. As I continued to research the Angle of Symmetry, I learned that repeating it successfully—the key to tapping its power—was dependent on grip size and stance width, the other two balance silver bullets (and two parts of your setup that I'm sure you've never thought twice about). It launched a whole new subset of studies designed to accurately determine these measurements on a golfer-by-golfer basis. The results led to the most personalized custom-fitting program the golf world has seen (www.gripsize.com).

**5 Things I'll Teach You In This Chapter**

**1** The importance of stance width and how to find one that's right for you.

**2** Why grip size is critical, and how to fit your flatstick to match your body.

**3** How to find your Angle of Symmetry (it's easier than you think).

**4** How to build your Angle of Symmetry into your stance for better balance and putt control.

**5** How the right stance width, grip size and the Angle of Symmetry give you a better view of your line.

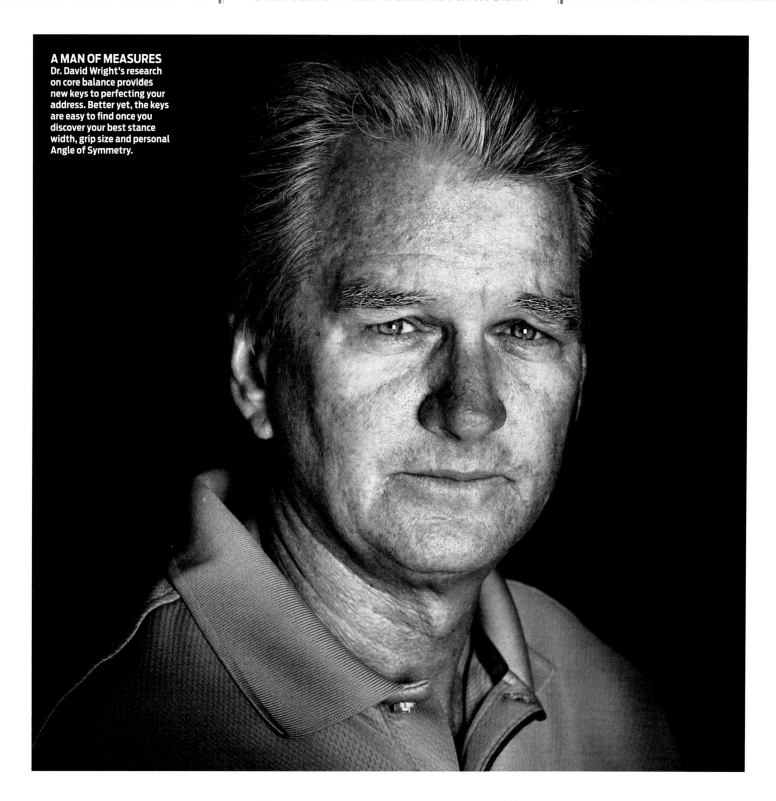

**A MAN OF MEASURES**
Dr. David Wright's research on core balance provides new keys to perfecting your address. Better yet, the keys are easy to find once you discover your best stance width, grip size and personal Angle of Symmetry.

## ALL ABOUT ME

**Name:**
David F. Wright, Ph.D.

**Teaching since:** 1982

**Where you can find me:** Wright Balance Golf Schools, Arroyo Trabuco G.C., Mission Viejo, Calif

**Where I've played:** Southern California mini-tours (1980s)

**Where I've taught:** Pelican Hill G.C. (Newport Coast, Calif.)

**Who I've instructed:** USC men's and women's golf teams (1999-2008); Kevin Stadler; Ramon Brobio

**Awards I've won:** So. Calif. PGA Teacher of the Year (1998); *GOLF Magazine's* Top 100 Teachers (2005-current); *GOLF Magazine's* Top 25 Golf Schools

**My best contribution to the game:** Discovery of individual biomechanics of balance

**For more instruction:** golf.com/ bestputtingbook gripsize.com wrightbalance.com

**Dr. Wright's research applies to all contact sports. Former MLB All-Star Reggie Smith teaches stance width and grip size at his elite batting clinics.**

## "We've developed a series of mathematical formulas to help you find your perfect stance width and grip size."

**T**O UNDERSTAND MY philosophy of putting, you have to understand that your stomach muscles (your "core") represent your body's center of gravity—they're ground zero for attaining balance and control in any motor action you execute. Problems arise when your core becomes imbalanced, a naturally occurring phenomenon in approximately 98 percent of the population. Core imbalance results from tension and, like the term suggests, forces you to favor one side of your body over the other. Sitting in a desk chair all day, working at a computer, driving in traffic and a variety of other activities contribute to the development of this problem. Even if you're a regular at your local gym, tension is always working against you.

When you don't have your center of gravity properly balanced at address (i.e., you have tension) your core muscles pull your hips either to the left or right, which affects both the weight dispersion in your feet and your ability to read the line of the putt accurately. In addition, if your hips are turned a bit open or closed at address, it's very likely you'll swing the putter along the same line, regardless of where you intend to start the ball. You're set up to fail even before you put your putter in motion.

I've spent a lot of time researching core imbalance, especially as it relates to your full swing and putting stroke. In addition to the daily tension-causing activi-

ties mentioned above, I found that balance can also be compromised by standing at address with your feet too far apart or too close together, or playing with grips that are either too small or too big for your hands. When these setup elements are off, your whole system falls out of whack. Luckily, my team has developed a series of mathematical formulas to help you find your perfect stance width and grip size so you can solve core imbalance problems—and the negative effects they have on your setup and stroke—for good. Before we begin, however, you should know a few things:

**1) YOUR STANCE WIDTH IS DETERMINED BY YOUR OVERALL BODY MASS,** and there's only one stance that will set you in balance when you putt.

**2) YOUR PERFECT GRIP SIZE IS BASED ON MEASUREMENTS OF BOTH HANDS.** Most of us have one hand that's slightly larger than the other so your grips should be sized to accommodate each.

Now for the real kicker: When you set up to putt with your correct stance width using a grip that fits both of your hands, you not only achieve better core balance, you also create a very specific angle in several key parts of your address. This Angle of Symmetry is very specific to you—it's as much a part of your DNA as your eye color or the freckles on your nose. I call it the Angle of Symmetry because it pulls the whole system together by giving you balance, an accurate perspective of your line and a weight distribution that allows you to swing your putter smoothly and on line.

Your Angle of Symmetry repeats itself twelve times in your address position when your stance width and grip size are accurate [see page 35]. Change one of these angles and your ability to swing the putter on your intended path and see the line accurately are compromised. Everything must work in tandem. When you get them right, however, you'll finally learn what great putters have always known—putting is *easy*.

**POSTURE PERFECT**
When your posture is correct—a state that includes a balanced core and the creation of the Angle of Symmetry in key parts of your body at address—holing putts becomes easy.

# THE IMPORTANCE OF PERFECT STANCE WIDTH

**EVERY GOLFER**, and every type of athlete for that matter (I instruct professional hockey, baseball and tennis players using the same research), has a correct, mathematically determined progression of stance widths that allows them to be perfectly in balance at address. This means that your feet are equally balanced on the ground, your arms are hanging freely and your eyes are in a neutral position to see your line of attack. When you take your address position with the wrong stance width, your body assumes an out-of-balance position that creates tension (tight muscles in your body's core). This leads to more flex in your right or left knee and a right or left rotation of your hips, depending on your body type.

This is all very bad stuff, but what's even worse is that an imbalanced address position makes it almost impossible to swing your putter in the direction you want—pretty alarming since we're talking about a very small movement made at a fairly slow pace. To understand this phenomenon, it's important that you become familiar with the terms Center Of Force (COF) and Line Of Force (LOF).

> **CENTER OF FORCE (COF):** The point in each foot where your weight is centered.
>
> **LINE OF FORCE (LOF):** A line connecting the COF in each foot. For most sports, the LOF should point in the same direction as the target you're hitting toward.

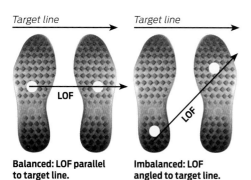

Target line

Target line

LOF

LOF

**Balanced: LOF parallel to target line.**

**Imbalanced: LOF angled to target line.**

**ONE FOR ALL**
There's only one stance width that allows you to set up in balance.

## WHY YOU NEED IT

When you're imbalanced (i.e., standing at your perfect stance width) your COF shifts from the center of both feet (where it likes to be when you're balanced) to either your heels or your toes. Often, the COF will be in the heel of one foot and the toe section of the other. This sets the LOF at an angle to your target line *[illustration, opposite page]*. If your LOF points to the left of your target (like it does when the COF in your left foot is in the heel and the COF in your right foot is in your toes), you'll swing your putter to your left. The opposite occurs when your LOF points to the right of the target line.

## HOW TO FIND IT

To determine if your current stance width is correct, begin by standing in front of a mirror. Take two credit or business cards and place them between your index and middle fingers *[photos, right]*. Assume your current stance width and place your palms together as though you're gripping your putter, with your right hand slightly lower than your left. From that position, relax your arms and hands and let them hang. At this point take notice of the orientation of the cards. If one of them turns in then you know your stance width is incorrect. Adjust your stance width until both cards point parallel to your target line. Once they do you'll know you're in the proper position.

## "An out-of-balance stance creates tension."

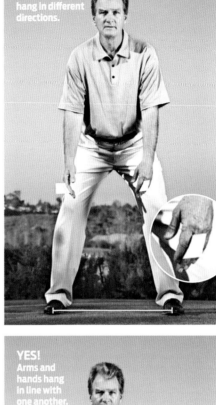

NO!
Arms and hands hang in different directions.

**INCORRECT STANCE WIDTH**
When I place business cards between my index and middle fingers and stand in an improper stance width, my left hand rotates inward.

YES!
Arms and hands hang in line with one another.

**CORRECT STANCE WIDTH**
When I move to my balanced stance width for a putter, notice how the cards are identical in how they set and how my arms and hands hang exactly the same. This is the balanced position that you're after.

# THE IMPORTANCE OF PERFECT GRIP SIZE

**WHEN YOU HOLD** something that fits your grip size for both your left and right hands, your core muscles remain balanced and your COF is centered in each foot (assuming, of course, you have a proper stance width). When you place something in your hands that's either too large or too small, core tension results and creates a left or right rotation of your hips, causing the COF to move forward in one foot and back in the other. Research shows that the grip size of most standard putters fits less than 5 percent of all golfers. Thus, 95 percent of you have a right or left hip rotation and a COF that's forward in one foot and back in the other.

**PULL**
A grip that's too small for your hands forces your right knee to over-flex and your hips to open. This putt's going left.

**PUSH**
A grip that's too big for your hands forces your left knee to over-flex and your hips to close. This putt's going right.

## TOO SMALL

Here I'm using a putter grip that's too small for both my left and right hands. Even though I'm set up in my balanced putting stance width, the grip size error causes my right knee to flex more than my left, forcing my hips to open up to my target. This moves the COF in my right foot to my toes, and the COF in my left foot toward the heel My putter path will track the resulting Line Of Force, which is outside-to-in with this particular grip size.

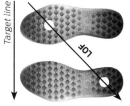

## TOO BIG

For this photo I've switched to a putter grip that's much too big for both my left and right hands. Notice that my left knee is now much more flexed than my right, and that the extra flex has forced my hips to close to the target line. As a result, the COF in my left foot has moved toward my toes, while the COF in my right foot has moved to my heel. This creates a Line Of Force that results in an inside-out putting stroke.

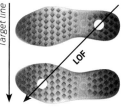

**CENTERED**
The correct grip size, coupled with the correct stance width, sets you up with perfect balance and aim.

**JUST RIGHT**
Here I'm using a putter grip that correctly fits both my right and left hands. Notice that the amount of flex is the same in both of my knees. My COF is in the same location in both feet, just behind the balls of each foot and just forward of the center of the arch. This Line Of Force sets me up for a path that's square to my target line.

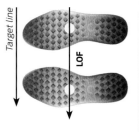

Target line

LOF

# BOTH HANDS MUST FIT

**HERE I HAVE** a grip that's the correct size for my left hand but too big for my right. Notice that when I have the putter in my left hand only *[top photo]*, my knee flex is the same and my hips are square. But when I add my right hand *[bottom photo]*, my left knee flex increases and my hips close.

Your putter grip must be fit to both your left and right hands. My left hand is about 100 mils (about 1/10 of an inch) larger than my right, so my putter grips have to be slightly tapered to fit my right hand.

To get an idea of the perfect grip size for your left and right hands, set a club on the ground parallel to your stance line and three or four inches away from your feet. Grip your putter and assume your setup. Notice if one knee extends farther out than the other using the shaft on the ground as a guide. If either does, then your current grip size is incorrect and you're establishing a LOF that doesn't match your target line. In other words, you're going to miss putts unless you make compensations in your stroke.

Take your grip with your left hand only...

...and if your posture changes when you add your right hand, you know you need tapered grips.

# THE IMPORTANCE OF THE ANGLE OF SYMMETRY

**ALL OF NATURE** has symmetry, whether you're looking at the rings of a pinecone or the petals of a sunflower. Symmetry and balance are synonymous. The way you build symmetry and balance into your setup and stroke is to tap a naturally occurring angle in your body that I call the Angle of Symmetry. This angle varies from individual to individual. It's part of you, embedded in your DNA and in your physique.

### HOW TO FIND IT
To locate your Angle of Symmetry, stand with your feet together and your arms hanging freely at your sides. Now, turn your palms so that they face directly away from you. Notice how this causes your forearms to angle away from vertical *[photo, right]*. This angle is your personal Angle of Symmetry, and it's entirely unique to you. It's the angle your body naturally creates to produce the most efficient and powerful motion.

**"Your Angle of Symmetry is part of you, embedded in your DNA."**

**SYMMETRY & BALANCE** My Angle of Symmetry is 152 degrees. Yours will be different. The Angle of Symmetry is unique for each individual.

Your Angle of Symmetry shows up here...

...and in your left and right thigh angle...

...in your spine angle as you bend forward...

..and in your shoulder tilt...

...in the angle of the shaft up each forearm...

...and in your left and right knee flex, plus four other places.

# HOW TO BUILD IT INTO YOUR ADDRESS

**YOUR ANGLE OF SYMMETRY** can easily be created by assuming a setup with a heavy weight held across your mid chest. This weight naturally sets your spine angle and thigh angle exactly the same as your measured Angle of Symmetry as you settle into your stance using your balanced stance width. The angle will show up in several parts of your setup, but only if your putter grip size fits both hands and if you're standing at your perfect stance width.

Notice in the photos above and at right how many times my Angle of Symmetry of 152 degrees is repeated in my setup (it actually shows up in 12 different places). From this position I have absolute balance and my putterface will remain square to the target line longer during my stroke than in any other address position. If you were to alter my grip size, posture or stance width, my Angle of Symmetry would begin to change and, as it changed, my putter path and face aim would move off the target line.

# HOW TO SET YOUR ANGLE OF SYMMETRY

**ON THE PREVIOUS** pages I showed you how to find your Angle of Symmetry and build it into your posture. The next step is to set it to your whole address, including the way you position your putter behind the ball.

I recommend you start setting this position with your grip. If you try to jump into your address position before doing so, there's a good chance you'll get it wrong from the start.

To begin, hold your putter in front of your body with your right hand on the shaft *[photo, below]*. Angle the shaft away from your body so it matches your Angle of Symmetry (once you practice with your Angle of Symmetry you'll get really good at eyeballing it). Now set your left hand on the grip.

Once you have this position correct, tilt the shaft to the right, again to match your Angle of Symmetry *[photo, right]*. For me, this places the putter shaft on a line close to my right ear. Now place your right hand on the grip as you normally would. Again, learning this position will take some practice, but once you do learn it, it'll become second nature.

After your grip and arms are solid, bring the putter down to the ground by bending your knees and hips so they also match your Angle of Symmetry. Obviously, you'll need the help of a friend or a mirror at first, but it won't take long for you to find your Angle of Symmetry positions on your own.

**STEP 2**
Tilt the shaft to the right the same number of degrees as your Angle of Symmetry.

**STEP 3**
Bend your hips and knees and sole the club on the ground.

**STEP 1**
Angle the shaft away from you the same number of degrees as your Angle of Symmetry.

# BALANCE AND PERSPECTIVE

**ANOTHER MAJOR SIDE** effect of an out-of-balance address position is an inability to see the line of a putt correctly. By being forced into an unnaturally open or closed stance your perception of the ball, the line of the putt and the hole will be thrown off, sometimes significantly.

When you're in absolute balance your visual perception of the putting line is accurate because you're in a neutral position. Be careful here: If you assume a balanced stance width with a wrong grip size, your perception of the line will be inaccurate and the putterface will aim left or right of the target line. The same holds true if you assume a balanced stance width but get your Angle of Symmetry wrong. The key is to get all three things correct and to have your COF in the middle of each foot.

What I want you to do once you learn your proper stance width, grip size and Angle of Symmetry is to start using that combination to more accurately read the line. Try going behind your ball and facing the hole straight on (stand perpendicular to the target line). Assume your balanced address position with the putter on the ground *[photo, right]*. Now examine the line. You've probably never had this perspective before, but it's much more accurate than the view you're getting with your current technique. Decide what line you want to take to the hole and memorize it.

Now step to the ball as you normally would and again assume your balanced setup position. You should have a very clear idea of the line and be able to identify where to start the putt easily. Since you're in proper balance the line you swing the putter along should match the line you see with your eyes perfectly.

## "When you're in absolute balance your visual perception of the putting line is accurate."

**READ IN BALANCE**
Stand behind the ball using your correct stance width and with the putter soled on the ground for your best perspective of the line.

**BALANCED**
You'll see the line accurately.

**IMBALANCED**
You'll mis-read the putt and pick the wrong line.

# PUTTING IT ALL TOGETHER: GRIPSIZE.COM

**BY NOW YOU** should have a pretty good estimation of your perfect stance width, perfect grip size and your Angle of Symmetry. But like most things in golf, any errors in your measurements will be magnified on the course. The information in this chapter is designed to help you recognize the importance of the three most critical setup elements and give you a ballpark figure for each. As you can imagine, there's a lot more to this story, and also in the way you can pinpoint your stance width, grip size and Angle of Symmetry down to the inch, mil and degree, respectively.

Unlike most custom-fitting techniques that rely on static measurements, our methods for nailing each of these three critical setup variables are based on your entire build and physi-

cal tendencies. It took a team of mathematical experts to create specific formulas to generate ironclad values based on detailed analyses of golfers' physiques, balance patterns and standard core dimensions. If you're interested in nailing your setup factors for good, then I encourage you to visit www.gripsize.com. There you'll find a detailed synopsis of my research and carefully designed tools to start your full address-position assessment. There's a charge involved, but the return will be well worth your investment, especially when the majority of your putts start to fall.

> "Our methods for nailing the three setup variables are based on your entire build and physical tendencies."

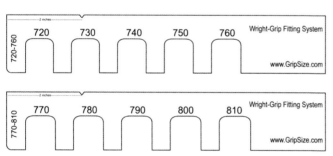

### GRIP CALIPERS
All of the research materials you need to measure your hands, grips and Angle of Symmetry can be found on www.gripsize.com.

### WWW.GRIPSIZE.COM
For less than the cost of 18 holes at your typical resort course, you can download several devices to perform a series of static measurements that, once entered into our online data form, allow our team to compute your perfect stance width, your perfect grip size and your Angle of Symmetry. Armed with these numbers you can create the ultimate address position—one that sets you up for putting success every time.

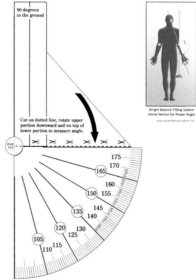

### PROTRACTOR
Download this tool to accurately measure your Angle of Symmetry in a matter of minutes.

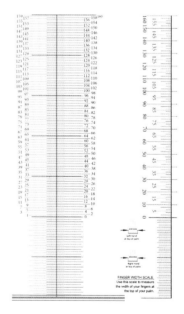

### HANDS
Our site offers step-by-step videos and documents to help you perform accurate left- and right-hand measurements.

**MANY OPTIONS, ONE FIT**
There's a wide variety of grip sizes and designs on the market. Our detailed program weeds them out and picks the right one for you.

# 3

# How to Calibrate
# Your Stroke

You have an internal tempo that's unique to you and that allows you to make solid strokes and control the distance on every putt. Here's how to find it, how to build it into your motion and adjust your stroke based on a very important factor—the type of putter you put into play.

# The Stroke Analyzer
# Mike Adams

*GOLF Magazine Top 100 Teacher, Hamilton Farm G.C., Gladstone, N.J./The Wanderers Club, Wellington, Fla.*

One of the most widely published instructors in the game shows you how to personalize your motion with a unique calibration method. The system allows you to tap your natural putting style instead of forcing you to repeat mechanics that your mind and body refuse to accept.

**W**HEN I FIRST started teaching putting in 1978 I was very concerned with the stroke—the myriad ways to swing that funny little club back and forth to roll the ball specific distances and to even more specific targets. It didn't take long to realize that stroke mechanics—while supremely important—aren't the be-all, end-all secret to holing more putts. The reason why is that there are several very good ways to swing your putter and achieve excellent results (see Chapters 4 and 5 for two popular options), and the best way for you to do it has absolutely nothing to do with how I putt, how your favorite Tour pro putts, or the methods that the members of your regular foursome use to take money from you on the greens. Rather, the best way for you to putt is to look at yourself.

Putting is personal—we all have a unique tempo and rhythm. Moreover, we prefer certain putters (the blunt instrument, not the one wielding it) over others, and we move our bodies in ways that feel good to us, which are often different from what you see on TV. These facts alone helped me switch my teaching philosophy from a universe-based approach to a more personal method, with the goal of developing techniques to assess students' stroke and putter preferences and match them to time-proven methods for rolling the ball into the hole with ease. As you'll read in this chapter, mission accomplished.

**5 Things I'll Teach You In This Chapter**

**1** How to find your natural stroke pace and tempo.

**2** How to calibrate your stroke to control distance on every putt.

**3** How to match your setup and stroke to the type of putter you use.

**4** How to analyze your putter to select the best stroke type for you.

**5** Where to play the ball in your stance based on your stroke preferences—an oft-forgotten fundamental.

**PACE MAKER**
Top 100 Teacher Mike Adams'
step-by-step guide to
calibrating your stroke starts
with finding your personal
tempo—the pace at which you
naturally stroke putts. Once
you get this down, you'll be
able to roll the ball close from
any distance using mechanics
that not only adhere to time-
proven fundamentals, but
also feel good to you.

**Adams' LAWs (with TJ Tomasi and Jim Suttie) is a must read.**

## "Good putters use the same pace on every stroke. More important, they use the pace wired into their system."

**H**ERE'S A FACT about the putting stroke that may surprise you: It takes the same amount of time to stroke a 35-foot putt as it does a 5-foot putt. In other words, the time from the start of your backstroke to impact is the same whether you need to roll the ball 5 feet, 35 feet, or any other distance. If you're like most of my students you're wondering, "How can that be? A longer putt requires a longer stroke, which takes longer to complete." Well, you have half of it right. Yes, a longer putt requires a longer stroke, but it's also a faster stroke, so it's not officially slower on the clock. The key ingredient here is pace—the rate of speed at which an activity or movement proceeds. Good putters use the same pace on every stroke, from long-range lags to short knee-knockers. More important, they use the pace that's naturally wired into their system.

Every player has his own unique pace—a tempo fingerprint. The pace at which you naturally make a stroke is different than the pace I use to stroke putts. It's also different from the pace Tiger uses, your neighbor uses—whoever. The secret to putting well is to find this personal rhythm and then work it into your motion. You can't avoid it because 1) your personal pace is a strong part of who you are, and 2) if you do you'll be forced to make compensations in your stroke—compensations that are difficult to time and that always result in bad

misses. To understand the concept of personal putting pace, think of a classic Type A individual at your work, the guy chugging coffee all morning and going about his business at breakneck speed. Now, picture him putting. What kind of stroke do you think he'll use? You can bet that it'll be as rapid-fire as his work pace. Next, think of the mellowest person you know and imagine his stroke. Getting the picture now?

Over the next several pages you're going to learn how to discover your personal putting pace and rhythm and, more important, how to apply it to the strokes you make out on the course. This is the first part (steps 1-4) of a five-step process that I call "calibrating your stroke," or, in other words, assessing your motion so that you can tap into your inherent skills.

The second part (step 5) involves building your inherent skills into your stroke based on another personal trait: the type of putter you use. While there may not be a perfect putter for you (if you're like a lot of golfers you own a closet full of misbehaving flatsticks), there is a perfect *type*, and if you've been playing for a long time then it's probably already in your hands, or sitting in that closet of yours waiting for a second chance. There's a reason why you choose certain types of putters over others, especially given the glut of options at your local pro shop: they just look and feel good to you. (If you aren't sure if you have the right instrument, consult David Edel's advice on putter selection in Chapter 1). The trick is to adapt your pace and stroke style to your preferred putter type. Once you do this, your putts will start dropping like crazy.

## CALIBRATION STEPS

**1.** Discover your natural putting pace and apply it to your motion.

**2.** Apply key setup and stroke changes to match your preferred putter type.

**TEMPO IS KING**
The pace of your stroke is personal—it's part of your putting DNA. Discovering this pace is absolutely critical for putting success.

The time you need to complete this short stroke...

...is the same amount of time you need to complete this mid-range stroke...

...which is the exact amount of time you need to complete this lag-putt stroke.

**TIME OUT**
Average out the number of steps you take over a 45 second time period in 5 trials to determine your personal tempo.

# STEP 1: FIND YOUR PERSONAL TEMPO

**THE FIRST STEP** in calibrating your stroke is to discover at which pace you should naturally swing your putter. The answer, of course, is at the tempo that's wired into your system—your personal pace of going about most of the motor actions you execute in a day. The most common of these activities is the simple act of walking, which you subconsciously do at your innate tempo. Your natural gait is a window to how fast or slow you like to move, and luckily there's an easy way to measure your walking tempo so that you can then apply it to your putting stroke.

## HOW TO DO IT
You'll need a friend and a stopwatch for this one (or any wristwatch with a second hand).

Find a flat section of ground and simply walk around. Have your friend time you for 45 seconds and count the number of steps you take during that time frame. At the end of 45 seconds, tally the steps and repeat. Do this five times, then compute your average pace count *[sidebar, right]*. That number is a concrete representation of your tempo.

I highly suggest you purchase a metronome (you can pick one up at any music store, or download one of several very good apps for your smart phone) and set it to your number. Then, listen—"ticktock, ticktock." Get a feel for the rhythm of your natural tempo. As you do, think of your backstroke as the "tick" and impact as the "tock." The timing and pace of this rhythm should feel very good to you.

**TEMPO TEST**
Find your personal putting tempo by counting the number of steps you take over the course of 45 seconds. The number is a very good indicator of the pace at which you like to execute most motor actions, including swinging your putter.

| | |
|---|---|
| *Trial 1* | 76 Steps |
| *Trial 2* | 72 Steps |
| *Trial 3* | 73 Steps |
| *Trial 4* | 78 Steps |
| *Trial 5* | 76 Steps |
| **Total** | **375 steps / 5 = 75** |
| | YOUR PERSONAL TEMPO |

# STEP 2: APPLY YOUR PERSONAL TEMPO TO YOUR STROKE

**EVEN THOUGH YOUR** personal tempo is a natural part of who you are, it'll take some work to make it a part of your putting stroke. Here's an easy way to do it. You'll need your metronome (set to your personal tempo number) and two small blocks of wood.

**STEP 1**

Anchor the two blocks of wood to the green with some tees, setting one a few inches outside your right foot and the other where you play the ball in your stance *[photo, right]*. Take your stance and begin swinging your putter back and forth, striking each block on successive beeps from the metronome. It helps to count in your head "1-2, 1-2" as you strike the blocks in time with the sound of the metronome. This is the pace you need to swing your putter for all putts.

**STEP 2**

Lengthen the distance between the blocks by moving the one on the right a solid foot and half outside your right foot *[photo, above]*. Repeat the drill, again making sure to strike each piece of wood on successive beeps. Notice that even though this is a longer stroke (for, obviously, a longer putt), it takes the same amount of time to complete as the shorter stroke in step 1. Two different-length putts executed at the same pace—perfect.

**STEP 3**

Remove the block on the left and replace it with a ball *[photo, above]*. Your goal this time is to strike the block on your right on one beep and the ball on the next. Usually, introducing a ball into this drill typically forces players to lose the pace they grooved in steps 1 and 2. This step will take the longest to complete, but stick with it. By the time you master this step, you should already be seeing an improvement in the quality of your roll.

# STEP 3: MATCH YOUR TEMPO TO PUTT LENGTH

**NOW THAT YOU** have your personal putting tempo and have begun cementing it into your stroke, the next step in my calibration system is to find out how your tempo relates to distance and speed. If, for example, your personal putting tempo is 76, your putts will travel farther than those made by someone whose tempo is 72 on equal stroke lengths. So it's important to know just how much distance you generate at varying stroke lengths. Here's how to do it.

### DO THIS: PACE DRILL
Place a dozen balls on a flat section of the putting green. Use tees to anchor four 8-foot-long pieces of string to the green, setting the first one 15 feet from the balls, the second 25 feet the balls, the third at 35 feet and the fourth at 45 feet *[illustration, below]*. Set your metronome at your personal tempo and putt the first three balls to the far string. Be sure to make your strokes to the beat of the metronome. Putt the next three balls to the 35-foot string and the last six to the two closest strings in succession. What you're doing is getting a feel for how long your stroke has to be to roll the ball specific distances using your natural tempo. (If you have time, perform a quick version of this drill on the practice green of the course you're playing that day to fine-tune your stroke for the speed of the greens you're about to play).

**GET THIS!**
A metronome is the best putting aid I can think of. It's your gateway to finding and grooving your personal putting tempo.

**DIALING IT IN**
Hitting balls to specific distances using the Pace Drill is an easy way to match your tempo to varying putt and stroke lengths.

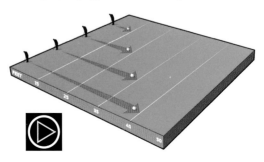

After you putt the twelve balls, reverse the lengths—hit three balls to the closest string first, and then the others in succession, three balls at a time. Then set up the strings so that you're putting uphill, and finally perform the drill on a downhill section of the green. After a few go-rounds with this drill, you'll own an inventory of stroke lengths to match just about any putt you face.

**"What you're doing is getting a feel for how long your stroke has to be to roll the ball specific distances."**

# STEP 4: TAKE YOUR PERSONAL TEMPO TO THE COURSE

**THE PREVIOUS STEP** in the calibration process helped you build an inventory of stroke lengths to roll the ball specific distances with your natural tempo. Good putters, however, don't rely on stroke length to roll the ball different distances, especially when they're out on the course. Rather, they feel it, based on what they're eyes tell them and how they judge the speed of the green. The following drill will help you do exactly that.

**FEEL YOUR WAY**
Your eyes see the target. Your mind uses that information to tell your body how much energy is necessary to hit the putt the correct distance.

**IMPORTANT!**
This step in the calibration method isn't just a drill. Make your practice strokes on the course standing at, ahead or behind the ball according to the slope. Remember: This method won't work if you don't focus your eyes on the hole when you make your practice strokes.

### STEP 1
Again, set your metronome on the ground near your feet and dial in your personal putting tempo. Find a downhill putt and set your ball about 15 feet from the hole [photo, above]. Instead of standing next to the ball to make your practice strokes, make them while standing a few feet closer to the hole on the same line as you take your putting stance. Important—make your practice strokes while looking at the hole. Then, go back to the ball and roll the putt.

### STEP 2
Switch to an uphill 15-foot putt. This time, take your practice strokes while looking at the hole from a few steps behind the ball to gauge stroke length and distance.

### STEP 3
Next, find a flat putt. When you go to make your practice strokes while looking at the hole, do so while standing next to the ball.

Your eyes are the windows to your mind, so making practice strokes while looking at the hole allows you to internally program your putting stroke to produce the exact length and distance you need. The reason why you stand closer to the hole on downhill putts and further from the hole on uphill putts is to adjust for the fact that downhill putts move faster and uphill putts move slower, mandating shorter stroke lengths and longer stroke lengths, respectively.

**ARC STROKE**
In an arc stroke, the putter swings to the inside of the target line on the backstroke...

...returns to square at impact...

...then swings to the inside in the through-stroke. This is the preferred stroke if you prefer blade- or Anser-style putters.

## THE MORE THE TOE SECTION OF YOUR PUTTER HANGS TOWARD THE

**FULL TOE HANG**
Old-school blade putters require max rotation and arc.

**3/4 TOE HANG**
Less arc than a blade, but still requires ample rotation.

**1/2 TOE HANG**
A popular style (made famous by the PING Anser) designed for an arc-like stroke.

# STEP 5: MATCH YOUR STROKE TO YOUR PUTTER

**MATCHING YOUR STROKE** to your personal putting tempo is an important first step. Now comes the million-dollar question: what kind of stroke should you use? For years, putting instructors have waged war over whether players are best served by an arcing stroke (where the putter moves slightly to the inside on the backstroke, back to square at impact, and then back to the inside on the through-stroke), or a pendulum stroke, in which the goal is to keep the putter-face square to the target line from start to finish. Theories abound: use an arc stroke if you stand tall to the ball or play on fast greens; use a pendulum stroke if you hunch over the ball or putt on slow greens. What really dictates the kind of stroke you should use is the type of putter you put into play. A putter's design does more than present a feel, sound or look. It facilitates a certain type of stroke, based on its shape, weight distribution and hosel configuration.

## GROUND...THE MORE ARC YOU NEED TO BUILD INTO YOUR STROKE

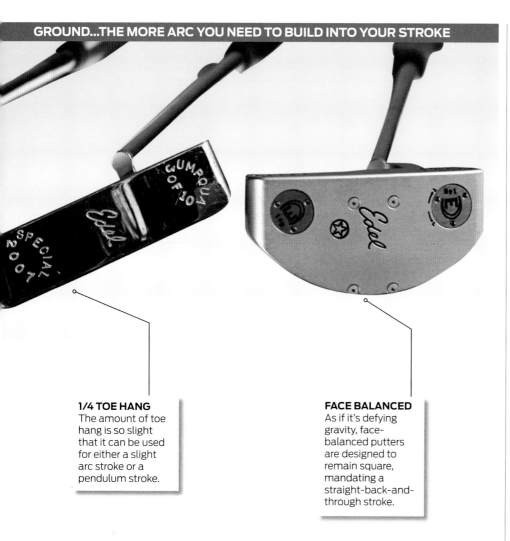

**1/4 TOE HANG**
The amount of toe hang is so slight that it can be used for either a slight arc stroke or a pendulum stroke.

**FACE BALANCED**
As if it's defying gravity, face-balanced putters are designed to remain square, mandating a straight-back-and-through stroke.

**PENDULUM STROKE**
In a classic pendulum stroke, the putter moves straight back on the backstroke (or on a very slight arc)...

...maintains its straight path back to impact...

...and continues straight through once contact has been made with zero face rotation. This is the preferred stroke if you prefer large face-balanced mallets.

If you prefer a large, face-balanced mallet or similarly shaped putter, use a pendulum-type stroke (and consult Maggie Will's advice in Chapter 5 for details). The reason? A large, face-balanced mallet is designed to keep the face from rotating during the stroke, thanks largely to the hosel shape (the face always wants to point where you have it aimed). If the instrument is designed to limit face rotation, then it makes sense that your stroke should, too.

If you prefer blade- or Anser-style putters, or models that feature significant toe hang, use an arc stroke (and heed Stan Utley's advice in Chapter 4). These kinds of flatsticks are designed to rotate because of the hang. To check how much toe hang is designed into your putter, balance it on your index finger just above the hosel. The amount of hang will vary from design to design, but even if it's just a few degrees, you'll know that the putter was built to be used with an arcing stroke.

# HOW TO SET UP FOR A PENDULUM STROKE

**IF YOU PREFER** to use a face-balanced putter, follow these address instructions to set your body and club for a solid straight-back-and-through stroke.

### STEP 1
Position the ball so that it's forward of center in your stance. This ball position aligns your shoulders square to the target line, which is critical to swinging your putter straight back and through and holding your target line.

### STEP 1
Bend forward from your hips until your eyes are directly over the ball and target line. Your arms should hang directly underneath your shoulders. (Just like proper ball position, setting your arms directly beneath your shoulders allows you to swing your putter with minimal arc.) Once you're set, shuffle in your stance until you feel balanced over each foot. Check your setup in front of a mirror and make sure that the shaft and your forearms form a straight line (set up with the mirror on your left to check this view). Also, check that your right palm is facing down the line on which you want the ball to start.

---

**ANGLE REDUCTION**
The reason you're addressing the putt like this is that it creates a minimum number of angles. The more angles you create at setup, the more likely you'll swing your putter on an arc, which isn't a very good idea when you have a face-balanced putter in your hands.

---

**"The more angles you create at setup, the more likely you'll swing your putter on an arc."**

**RIGHT PALM**
Pointing down the target line.

**FEET**
Supporting your weight evenly, from the balls to the heels.

**PUTTERFACE**
Squared up to the target line.

**BALL**
Positioned just forward of center in your stance.

**EYES**
Directly over
your target line.

**SHOULDERS**
Square to the
target line (not
open or closed).

**ARMS**
Hanging directly
underneath your
shoulders.

**SHAFT**
In line with both
forearms.

# HOW DO I KNOW IF I'M USING THE RIGHT PUTTER?

**A LOT OF** the information in this chapter is based on the fact that you've chosen a particular putter because you like it. But what if you're not so sure? Here's an easy test to determine if the putter in your bag is indeed your putter of choice.

## DO THIS: TWO-BALL DRILL

Place two balls side-by-side flush against your putterface (it's vital that neither ball is closer to or farther from the hole than the other). Now, strike the putt. If the ball closest to the toe section of your putter rolls farther than the ball closest to the heel, you should use a toe-weighted putter, because you naturally rotated the face during your stroke (the toe struck first, sending the outside ball farther). On the other hand, if the ball closest to the heel section goes farther, or both balls travel the same distance, opt for a face-balanced putter. You naturally swing the putter with zero or negative face rotation.

**Hitting two balls at once tells you in an instant what type of stroke you should use.**

# HOW TO SET UP FOR AN ARC STROKE

**THE SETUP PROCEDURE** for a toe-weighted putter is a bit more complex. As a general rule, the less toe hang on your putter, the more you should play the ball back in your stance, like you do with a face-balanced mallet. Also, as the toe hang decreases, the more forward you should bend from your hips at address. Remember, the greater the hang, the more arc you need in your stroke, and you create more arc by standing taller and playing the ball forward in your stance.

**FULL TOE-HANG SETUP**
*Follow these rules for max arc and rotation.*

**BALL POSITION**
Play the ball way forward in your stance, off the logo on your shirt.

**POSTURE**
Stand more erect at address, so that your eyes are two inches inside the target line.

## 3/4 TOE-HANG SETUP
*Follow these rules for ample arc and rotation.*

## 1/2 TOE-HANG SETUP
*Follow these rules for medium arc and rotation.*

## 1/4 TOE-HANG SETUP
*Follow these rules for minimal arc and rotation.*

**POSTURE**
Bend slightly at address, with your eyes 1.5 inches inside the target line.

**BALL POSITION**
Play the ball forward in your stance, off your left ear.

**POSTURE**
Bend forward from your hips so that your eyes are one inch inside the target line.

**BALL POSITION**
Play the ball slightly forward of center, off the left side of your face.

**POSTURE**
Bend forward at address so that your eyes are just a half-inch inside the target line.

**BALL POSITION**
Play the ball near the center of your stance, off your left eye.

# 4
# Mastering the
# Arc Stroke

Most of the putters in your local pro shop are built to swing back and through on an arc. Not only does this help you get the most out of your putter's design, but it puts you in some great company—the majority of world-class putters move their flatsticks on an arcing path.

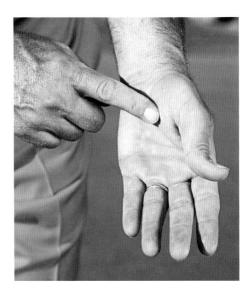

# The Tour Teacher
# Stan Utley

*Grayhawk Learning Center, Grayhawk G.C., Scottsdale, Ariz.*

When he competed on the PGA Tour, Stan Utley possessed one of the most envied strokes in golf. Now he's passing on his knowledge to create a new legion of flatstick magicians using the most time-proven stroke in the game: the arc stroke.

**T**HEY CALL PUTTING "the great equalizer," and I believe that's true. In fact, the only real reason I was able to compete on the professional level was because I could get the ball in the hole better than most people. In 2002 I played a full round at the Air Canada Open and finished with 21 putts, which included a PGA Tour-record 6 putts on the front nine. Imagine what would happen to your scores if you shaved just five strokes per round by making more one-putts and cutting out your three-putts. If you're open to making some changes to your existing technique, you'll be able to do it. Remember that you don't have to be a great physical athlete to be a solid putter. What you do need is a consistent, repeatable stroke that you can rely on every time you step on a green. That's what I've always focused on in my own game, and it's helped many of my students, including a number of very good PGA Tour players.

Pay close attention to the fundamentals I describe, particularly the grip, setup, and my stroke technique. Once you get these down, you'll be well on your way to being more relaxed with the putter in your hands, which is another important contributor to success on the green.

The bulk of my instruction is geared to what most putting instructors refer to as an arc stroke. If you tested out for an arc stroke based on your putter and stroke tendencies in Mike Adams' calibration process (Chapter 3), then pay close attention. These lessons will turn that sometimes-trusty putter of yours into a consistent thing of beauty.

## 5 Things I'll Teach You In This Chapter

**1** The benefits of the Tour-proven arc stroke.

**2** How to grip your putter and set up to make the smoothest arc possible.

**3** How to align properly at address so you get your putts started on the right line.

**4** How to feel the arc in your stroke so you can repeat it consistently.

**5** How to practice an arc stroke using unique training aids.

**ATTENTION, PLEASE!**
When former PGA Tour player Stan Utley talks about putting, and in particular, the arc stroke, dozens of Tour players and his growing stable of elite students listen.

## ALL ABOUT ME

**Name:** Stan Utley
**Teaching since:** 1999
**Where you can find me:** Grayhawk Learning Center, Grayhawk G.C., Scottsdale, Ariz.
**Where I've played:** University of Missouri (three-time All-Big 8 and three-time All-American selection); Nationwide Tour (3 victories); PGA Tour (1 victory)
**Who I've instructed:** Jay Haas, Peter Jacobsen, Sergio Garcia, Paul McGinley, Darren Clarke, Rocco Mediate, Dudley Hart, Alex Noren, D.A. Points, Kevin Streelman and Henrick Stenson, among others
**Awards I've won:** *Golf Magazine's* Top 100 Teachers (2009-current); *Golf Digest's* America's 50 Greatest Teachers (#6)
**My best contribution to the game:** Author of three best-selling instruction books: *The Art of Putting*, *The Art of the Short Game* and *The Art of Scoring*
**For more instruction:** golf.com/ bestputtingbook stanutley.com

# "I like to think of the putting stroke as swinging in a circle on a tilt—like a miniature version of your full swing."

**T**HE METHOD THAT I teach, which is based on the arc stroke, is basically the one that has worked for me since I learned it in junior high. My teacher at the time, a famous amateur from Missouri named Ken Lanning, believed that getting the fundamentals correct was the basis of good putting, and I spent a lot of time making sure I could repeat my grip, stance, posture and alignment over and over. That's something we're going to cover in this chapter, and if you listen to my advice and put your work in, you too will learn to get it right every time.

You might be reading this and saying to yourself, "Yeah, I've heard the fundamentals are important, but the good putters I know have great strokes, not setups." Well, it's true that great putters tend to make it look easy, and their strokes do often look great, but it's largely because of solid fundamentals that they appear so good. A proper grip allows the putterhead to swing naturally and release, which makes the stroke look effortless. And proper stance and alignment make it easy to get the ball rolling on the intended line without having to manipulate the hands or putterhead.

After you learn to get your fundamentals solid I'm going to teach you how to make an arcing stroke, the one the majority of putting greats have used and continue to put into play week after week on the PGA Tour. Now, I now that there are a lot of terrific players in the world

who keep the putterhead square to the line throughout their stroke and try to remove any semblance of arc in their motion, but this isn't the method I prefer to teach. Instead, I'll teach you how to swing the putter the same way you swing your other clubs, in a natural circular motion. This is especially true if, like Mike Adams pointed out in Chapter 3, you prefer to play with a putter that features toe hang, which is designed to be swung on an arc. (If you prefer a face-balanced mallet or feel more comfortable with a straight-back-and-through stroke, then by all means consult Maggie Will's advice in Chapter 5).

I like to think of the putting stroke as swinging in a circle on a tilt—like a miniature version of your full swing. That's how I putt and how I want you to start putting. In my opinion, the arc stroke imparts the purest roll and heightens your sense of feel on the greens—something that good players never take for granted since they must constantly adjust for green speed week in and week out. Once you perfect the arc stroke, there will be no looking back.

## LEARNING THE ARC STROKE

**1.** Perfect your grip—you need a tension-free hold so that the putter can "release" freely.

**2.** Nail your stance and alignment—even the best arc stroke won't work if you're pointed in the wrong direction.

**3.** Learn the motion—it sounds difficult, but it's the most natural stroke you can make.

## WATCH & LEARN

 When you see this icon, go to to **golf.com/ bestputtingbook** for a video lesson with Top 100 Teacher Stan Utley.

**ARC IN MOTION** The arcing stroke moves in a circular shape, just like a full swing, both forward and through and with the toe of the putter "releasing."

  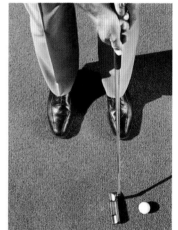 

**FACE FACT** It may look like the face is opening and closing, but it isn't. The face remains square to the arcing path from start to finish.

# ARC-STROKE FUNDAMENTALS: THE GRIP

**WHEN I TEACH** amateurs, the one thing most of them have in common is tension. Their arms and hands are tight and it spreads to their shoulders and throughout their entire body. To begin putting well you need to release tension from your body and feel natural. This starts with your grip.

When I say "natural" I mean the positions to which your body would return to in its passive state. If your body were at rest you wouldn't have your arms tight or your elbows bent or a whole lot of tension in your shoulders. Instead your arms would hang down freely with your elbows just slightly bent, and your hands would be soft and relaxed. This is what you should feel in your putting grip. You need to have your hands on the putter in a neutral position, which to me is the same as natural.

## GRIP BASICS

The first thing you need to do to attain a proper grip is to make sure your hands are facing one another. The back of your left hand and the palm of your right hand should be square to the target line. The most common mistake I see from my amateur students is that they get the left hand too weak. This error tends to cause the player to open the putterface through impact. Also, make sure your thumbs come to rest on the top of the putter grip, not down the sides.

Unlike a full shot, where you want to hold the grip in your fingers, for putting you need it in your palms. This places the shaft of the putter in line with your forearms. You don't need the same wrist hinge for putting that you need for a full shot. Putting is about control, not distance, and getting the shaft of the putter lined up with your forearms is critical to swinging the putter on the proper plane.

## LOOSEN IT UP

I prefer a reverse-overlap grip for putting with the index finger of the left hand resting on top of the knuckles of the right hand *[inset photo, right]*. If you place the handle of the club properly in the palms of your hands and use this grip, you'll feel like your grip is fairly loose. This is a good thing. I want you to feel relaxed and "soft" with your grip, not tight. This combination also puts the handle of the club more in touch with your fingertips, which are some of the most sensitive parts of your body.

## LEVEL FOREARMS

The other benefit of this type of grip is that it puts your forearms in a level position. If you get your left forearm higher than your right you're going to have the tendency to swing the putterhead too far to the inside. The opposite occurs if you position your left forearm lower than your right. Making sure your forearms are evenly aligned will eradicate these mistakes and make you a lot more consistent.

**HANDS**
Your palms should oppose one another so the palm of your right hand and the back of your left hand are both facing the target line.

# THE ARC GRIP: STEP-BY-STEP

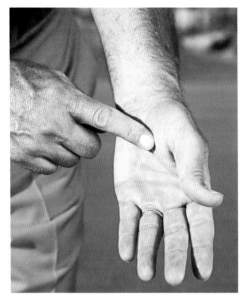

**STEP 1:** The lifeline of your left hand is key. Unlike a full shot you don't want the grip to be held in your fingers.

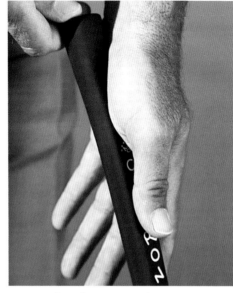

**STEP 2:** Place the grip squarely in the palm of your left hand so it runs right up the lifeline. This will position the shaft in line with your forearms.

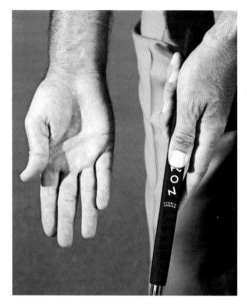

**STEP 3:** Make sure that your left thumb runs straight down the top of the grip, not down the side.

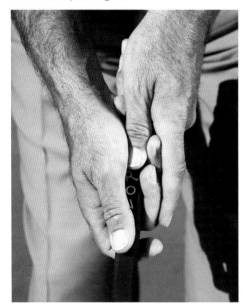

**STEP 4:** Place your right hand on the grip so that the index finger of your left hand rests on the knuckles of your right. This is a reverse-overlap hold, and I highly recommend it.

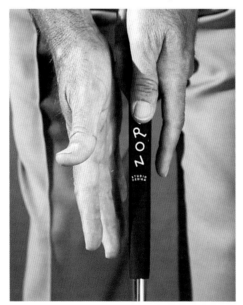

**STEP 5:** Check that your right and left palms oppose one another. Your right palm must face the target, just like the back of your left hand.

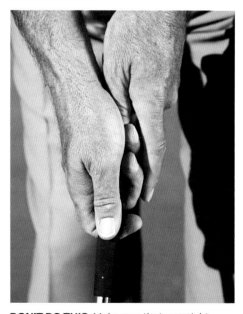

**DON'T DO THIS:** Make sure that your right thumb pad is on top of the grip, not your right lifeline. Getting too much of your right hand on top of the grip sets your right arm too high.

# ARC-STROKE FUNDAMETALS: THE SETUP

**MASTERING A SOUND** address position starts with stance width. If your stance is currently very wide or extremely narrow, you probably don't feel comfortable and your balance probably isn't very good. You should place your feet no wider than shoulder-width, and you should feel balanced. If this still feels too wide, you should narrow your stance a bit. With your feet closer together your shoulders will be better able to rotate with the stroke.

## FORWARD TILT

Once you get a comfortable stance I want you to tilt forward from your hips, again in a comfortable position. You don't want to slump over with a bent spine because this position will inhibit the movement of your elbows and your stroke will become too handsy. Standing with your back ramrod straight isn't good either, because it will tend to make your stroke more up and down than rotational. Just bend from your hips until the putter is soled comfortably on the ground. You shouldn't feel locked up or awkward in any way, but instead you should feel totally at ease.

## SETTING SHAFT ANGLE

Another simple but key aspect of a solid setup is shaft angle. I can't tell you how many players I see who set up with the shaft leaning much too far forward, toward the target, or much too far back, away from the target. Between the two, leaning the shaft away from the target is much worse. If you do this, I can pretty much guarantee you won't be able to make solid contact with the ball. I like to forward-press (lean the shaft toward the target) just a bit, because it encourages the putterhead to move away from the ball first, instead of the handle of the club. Just don't overdo it.

## BALL POSITION

Finally, make sure your ball position is correct. Too far back and you'll tend to miss to the right, too far forward and you'll hit a lot of pulls. My advice is to start with the putterhead in the middle of your feet. Place the ball in a position just ahead of this spot, which would

**POSTURE**
Bend from your hips. You shouldn't feel slumped or too rigid.

**WEIGHT**
Evenly distributed between your feet.

**NO!**
If your right forearm peeks out above or below your left forearm (check this in a mirror), then you have major alignment problems.

place it slightly forward of the middle of your stance. Though this might not seem like a big deal, it's an important fundamental.

A good way to tell if you're set up correctly at this point is to check your eye position. Your eyes should be just inside the golf ball. I also suggest you place your left eye slightly behind the ball (as in away from the target). To check this, assume your stance, place a ball over your left eye, and drop it. It should land just inside and just behind the ball on the ground. I know this is an old trick, but it's something a lot of players get wrong. Make this a regular part of your practice until you can get it right.

**SHOULDERS**
Level, with your right shoulder a bit lower than your left.

**ARMS**
Elbows relaxed and close to your body.

**BALL POSITION**
Ball positioned just forward of center.

**STANCE**
Feet shoulder-width or narrower.

**DISTANCE FROM BALL**
Eyes inside and behind the ball.

**SHAFT ANGLE**
Clubshaft in line with your forearms and angled slightly toward the target.

# ARC-STROKE FUNDAMENTALS: DEVELOPING FEEL

**AS PREVIOUSLY DISCUSSED**, the basis of my philosophy on putting is the arcing stroke. This is one that moves slightly to the inside on the backstroke to square through the ball and back to slightly inside on the through-stroke. Think of it the same way you would a full golf swing. The only difference is that the putting stroke is smaller and less forceful. To make a solid arcing stroke you need to let the toe of the putter pass the heel past impact. It may feel a bit like you're hooking the ball.

There are a fair number of good players who try to hold the putter square to the target line all the way through the stroke. To me this isn't the most natural way considering that the entire game of golf is played with a circular motion. What I want you to do is swing the putter on the shaft plane, not on the target line. If you do this, the putterhead will naturally trace a more circular route and you won't have to manipulate it to make it go inside on the backstroke or release past impact.

To make a good arc stroke you need to keep tension to a minimum and swing freely. Learn to make the stroke with soft elbows, wrists and arms. You should never feel that your arms are locked or that your shoulders are driving the motion. I know a lot of you have been taught this move, but all it really does is make your stroke stiff and rigid. When I putt I actually let my arm-swing move my shoulders instead of the other way around. The following drills will help you ingrain this important feel.

**A TENSION-FREE STOKE** Swing your putter at waist height without moving your shoulders. This is the correct feel—your arms drive your arc stroke.

## DO THIS:
### ROTATION DRILL
Assume your setup and raise your arms so the putterhead is out in front of your belly button [photo, above left]. Don't extend your arms out away from your body in a rigid position but instead let your elbows bend softly and keep them close to your body. Now swing the putter around your body without moving your chest or shoulders much. To do this you need your right arm to bend in the backswing and your left arm to bend in the through-swing. Repeat this a number of times until you can really feel the weight of the putterhead swinging.

Now get in your normal setup and immediately try stroking some balls with the same method you used for the drill. You should feel much freer than normal and your stroke should seem fairly effortless. You might find that your distance control is a little off because you're not gripping the putter as tightly as normal but you'll soon adapt. Keep alternating between the drill and actually stroking balls until you can get the same sensation doing both.

> "What I want you to do is swing the putter on the shaft plane, not on the target line."

## THEN DO THIS: ONE-HAND DRILL

The goal with this exercise is to feel that the energy of your putting stroke is coming from the head of the putter, not the grip. The more you feel the putterhead through your stroke, the freer and more natural it will be.

To begin, place the putter in your right hand only and make a number of practice swings. Concentrate on really feeling the weight of the putterhead as it swings. Once you feel comfortable with a right-hand-only stroke, hit five or six balls with the same motion as your practice swings. Try to keep the top of the grip and your arm relatively still.

Next, switch hands and repeat the same drill with your left hand only. This will feel a bit different because you're effectively hitting a backhand instead of a forehand, but the idea is the same. After you get comfortable with this, place both hands on the putter and stroke some putts with the same motion you made while hitting one-handed. You should notice that your hands are now working together easily. You shouldn't have to try to swing the putterhead on an arc—it should happen on its own.

**THE NATURAL** Do this drill correctly and the putter will swing on an arc by itself without added manipulation.

**FEEL THE WEIGHT** Putt five or six balls one-handed to ingrain the feel of the weight of the putterhead tracing an arc both back and through.

# ARC-STROKE FUNDAMENTALS: MAKING IT HAPPEN

**BY NOW YOU'VE** corrected your grip, stance, alignment and ball position. You've done some drills to get the feel of the arcing stroke and you've released the tension from your arms, wrists, hands, and shoulders. It's time to start putting it all together and making a solid stroke.

Again, the important things to remember when you're making an arc stroke are that 1) you're not rotating the face open or closed but rather moving your putter on an arcing path with the face remaining square to your path from start to finish; 2) the energy for your stroke comes from your tension-free motion, not your shoulders; 3) you're as smooth and tension-free as possible, a state that allows you to feel the weight of the putterhead so that it can naturally trace an arc with the face remaining square to the path from start to finish; and 4) you swing your putter on the plane established by the puttershaft, not the actual target line. I recommend using my example as a model so you can see what the entire thing looks like.

> **"The energy for your stroke comes from your tension-free motion, not your shoulders."**

**1.** To begin, I assume my solid grip and stance, making sure my eyes are slightly inside the ball. Aligning your forearms with the shaft is a must (as is keeping your forearms level). You should feel comfortable and tension-free.

**2.** As you start your backstroke you should feel like you're moving the putterhead away from the ball, not the handle. Do it correctly and you'll feel the weight of the putterhead as it swings freely back and slightly inside.

**6.** If this were a six-inch putt I might only swing from here, but you can see that the putterhead would still swing on an arc. Keep in mind that no matter how small a stroke you make, your putter always swings in a circle.

**7.** Impact comes a bit from the inside, but since your putterface remains square to the path it's nice and square at the moment of truth. This imparts a slight hook spin, a critical element for a smooth roll that tracks the target line.

**3.** At this point in the backstroke you can clearly see that the putterhead has swung to the inside of the target line. I haven't pulled it inside consciously; I've allowed it to swing freely on the shaft plane, not the target line.

**4.** This is the most inside the putterhead should get. Notice how the toe of the putter is in line with the ball. To make contact in the center of the face I have to re-trace the path and keep the putterface square to it.

**5.** Players with too much tension in their hands, arms and shoulders often have trouble making a smooth transition from backstroke to forward-stroke. Keep your grip soft and your body relaxed, and you'll putt smooth every time.

**8.** Even after the ball begins tracking toward the hole it's very important to continue to swing the putter along the shaft plane, not down the target line. It's critical that you maintain the circular shape throughout your stroke!

**9.** My hands are working together nicely here. The palm of my right hand and the back of my left hand are moving together on the shaft plane. If you don't have your palms facing one another, they'll fight each other the whole way.

**10.** You'll probably notice the ball rolling out a bit more with this stroke, especially if you're used to cutting across the ball. That's because this stroke creates less sidespin and imparts a tighter and smoother roll with less "wobble."

# AN AID FOR WHAT AILS YOU

**A GREAT WAY** to ingrain the arcing stroke is to use a training aid like the Learning Curve (visit eyelinegolf.com for details). To utilize an aid like this, place the toe of your putter next to the device and make some practice strokes. If you don't have a good feel for the arcing stroke yet, you'll notice that your putter swings over the sections of the device where the curve begins *[photos, right]*. To remedy this problem try to feel as though you're swinging on the shaft plane, not the target line.

Pay attention to the hash marks on the Learning Curve. They're square to the arcing path, not the target line. These marks indicate where the putterhead should be aimed at various points in the stroke. If you can't get the feel of swinging on the shaft plane simply use your eyes to guide the putter to these hash marks. By feel or through these visual cues you should quickly get the feel of swinging on the proper arc.

Once you get the hang of the shape of the stroke *[sequence, far right]*, place a ball down and stroke a few putts with the help of the training device. You'll see that although you're swinging on an arc, the ball rolls nice and straight. It's important to believe that an arcing stroke will produce a straight roll, and this exercise will go a long way toward convincing you.

Keep in mind that this device is engineered for a putter with a 68-degree lie angle, which is fairly standard. If your putter is more upright, you'll need to create less arc; a flatter putter requires more arc.

## A FINAL NOTE

Remember that the toe of the putter must pass the heel in order to make a proper arc stroke. One of the most common errors for amateur players is leading with the heel. This mistake leads to both pushes and pulls. Think "hook" more than "slice" and you'll be on the right track.

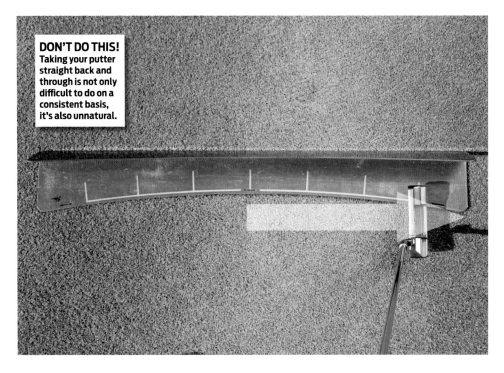

**DON'T DO THIS!** Taking your putter straight back and through is not only difficult to do on a consistent basis, it's also unnatural.

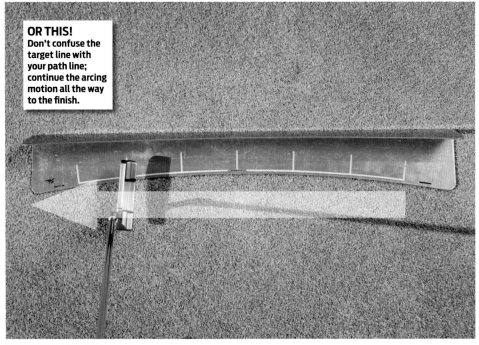

**OR THIS!** Don't confuse the target line with your path line; continue the arcing motion all the way to the finish.

**LEARN THE CURVE** A device like the Learning Curve tells you if you're making a correct arc stroke *[opposite page]* or a poor arc stroke, or one devoid of any arc at all *[above]*.

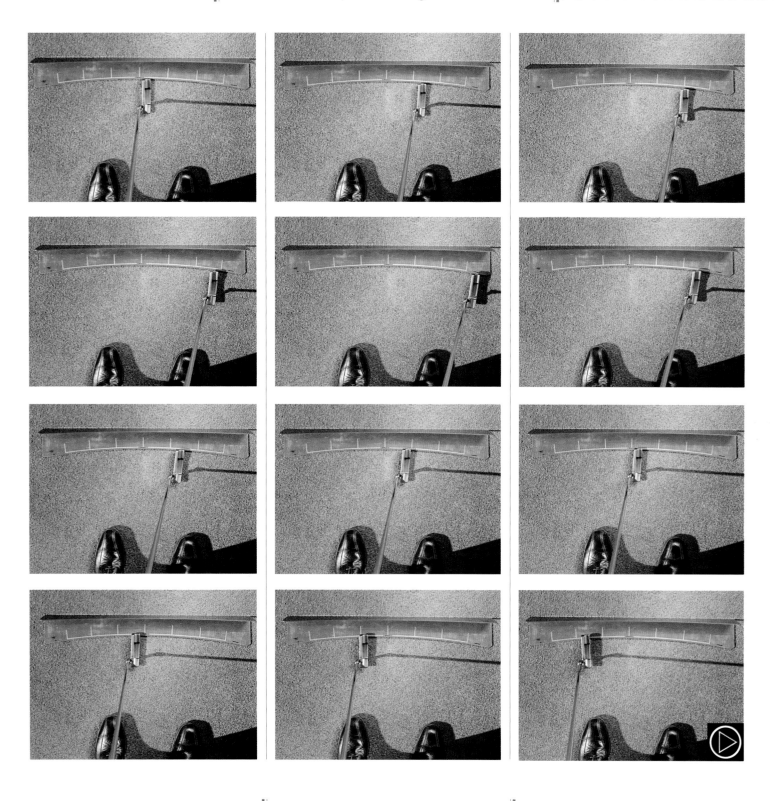

# 5
# Mastering the Brush Stroke

The pendulum stroke is touted as a more user-friendly alternative to the arc method, but it creates inconsistencies in contact when you don't strike the ball at the absolute bottom of your stroke. My new take on the pendulum—the Brush Stroke—eliminates these inconsistencies for good.

# The Stroke Pioneer
# Maggie Will

*LPGA Tour professional and instructor, Raleigh, N.C.*

A three-time winner on the LPGA Tour, insightful putting analyst, teacher and college golf coach Maggie Will identifies and clarifies common putting misconceptions and presents a new type of stroke to put you on track to far fewer putts per round

**I**'**VE STUDIED ALL** of the various theories in putting books and videos and assessed countless strokes of everyday players and professionals, and the one common thread is that everyone refers to the motion make with their putter as a putting "stroke." But what I see in photos and videos, and in person when I'm teaching, is more of a putting "swing," where the hands and the handle of the club are perpendicular to or behind the ball at impact rather than in front of it. This is the result of the "pendulum" theory and imagery of putting, and it produces very inconsistent results and requires perfect ball position every time you set up to putt. If your ball position is an iota off the mark, you're in trouble.

I believe the putting motion is literally a stroke, as if you're painting. and neither the arc method nor the pendulum action do a sufficient enough job of ingraining this feel. Think about how your hand and the handle of a paintbrush must always lead the actual bristles. If you flip your wrist forward and the bristles pass your hand in a flicking motion, what happens? Paint is scattered everywhere—just like your putts are when you employ a pendulum action and you make even the tiniest error in your setup or execution.

When you putt, the handle of the putter should be forward of the putterface at impact. When you do this, you eliminate almost all of the variables that make putting difficult. In this chapter I'll show you how, with a stroke culminated from years of experience playing, practicing and teaching that makes creating perfect roll easy and consistent.

**5 Things I'll Teach You In This Chapter**

**1** The difference between what you feel and what is real.

**2** Why the handle must lead your stroke.

**3** Why the pendulum stroke is the most misunderstood concept in golf.

**4** How to adjust your straight-back-and-through stroke to remove inconsistencies in contact.

**5** A new way to putt—the Brush Stroke.

**BRUSH WITH GREATNESS**
Maggie Will believes your putting stroke is just that—a stroke—and that it's more consistent and immune to many negative influences if the handle lead the stroke as if you were painting.

## ALL ABOUT ME

**Name:** Maggie Will
**Teaching since:** 2006
**Where you can find me:** Lonnie Pool G.C., Raleigh, N.C.
**Where I've played:** Furman University; LPGA Tour (3 wins: 1990 LPGA Desert Inn International, 1992 Sara Lee Classic, 1994 Children's Medical Center Classic)
**Where I've taught:** Creek Club (Locust Valley, N.Y.); Abacoa G.C. (Jupiter, Fla.)
**My best contribution to the game:** Translating lessons learned while playing and teaching to create a new method to roll consistent putts.
**For more instruction:** golf.com/bestputtingbook getfitforputting.com

My win at the 1990 LPGA Desert Inn Invitational was one of three I captured in blustery conditions—conditions that altered my approach to putting and led to the development of the Brush Stroke.

# "The effort wasn't producing satisfactory results. There had to be a better way. Turns out, I knew what it was all the time."

**I** HAD MY FIRST formal putting lesson the summer after I graduated from college. The gospel of putting in those days was simply that it was all about "feel" and that it was a "personal thing." The only way to get better at putting, it was believed, was the same way you get to Carnegie Hall. So there I was, a shag bag filled with 52 old practice balls and a tee in the ground one foot from the hole. The lesson: Make 52 putts in a row from a foot. Part two of the lesson: Move the tee back to two feet, and make 52 successive putts from that distance. After lunch, I was told to move the tee back to three feet. There was no thought behind what I was doing, and I was young and had time to practice hour after hour, so it worked. Sort of. The homemade stroke I grooved by rote was good enough to help me win three times on the LPGA Tour, but I was an inconsistent putter at best, struggling and frustrated for most of the time between those wins.

As my days on Tour were winding down, my curiosity grew stronger. Why was it so easy to get concrete and systematic advice on every aspect of the game except putting. While I was a pretty steady putter inside of six feet, I felt I could be better from 10 to 20 feet and make more birdies. Most of the time I came up short and right on my mis-hit putts. Other times, after frustration had set in, I hit the power switch and jammed it long and left, something that might sound familiar to you. If you'd asked me at the time I would have said I took the putter straight back and straight through, but

careful analysis showed that my stroke went outside on the way back, then looped back to the inside with a lot of manipulation through impact to keep the face from rotating to the left. What I learned was that what you feel and what is real are often totally different. If I could have continued to manipulate the putter successfully, I would have never looked for another way to putt. But the effort I was making was not producing the results I wanted. I was getting older and less capable of making the manipulations at the precise moment. I could sense the yips coming on. There had to be a better way. Turns out, I knew what it was all the time.

Looking back on it all I realized that I did something unique in each of my three LPGA Tour victories as well as on my other good putting days. It begged a question: "Why do I make so many putts in windy conditions?" I know I'm a grinder, but there was more to it than that. The link is that in order to combat the wind I altered my address position. I widened my stance, I crouched into a more hunched position and face-down setup, and I lifted the handle of the putter more toward vertical to keep it from getting caught in my wind jacket. The end result of these alterations was that I was more steady over the ball because of the wider stance, the line to the hole lit up because my face-down position set my eyes more on plane with the putting surface, and setting my puttershaft more toward vertical caused me to grip the putter under my thumb pads instead of my heel pads, which reduced face rotation almost to nil.

These are the hallmarks of my putting stroke that I call the Brush Stroke and, like it has done for me, it will help you sink more putts.

## BRUSH-STROKE BASICS

**1.** Crouched stance, eyes and head over putt line.
**2.** Wrists bowed, hands pointed down.
**3.** Handle forward through impact.

## WATCH & LEARN

 When you see this icon, go to to **golf.com/bestputtingbook** for a video lesson with LPGA professional Maggie Will.

**A BETTER WAY**
My face- and body-down approach to putting gives you the best view of your line. When you pair it with a grip that places the handle under your thumb pads, and are successful in keeping the handle ahead of the putterface through impact, you'll start draining putts like crazy.

# THE PROBLEM WITH ARCS

**TRADITIONALLY, THE PUTTING** stroke has been taught as a simultaneous (but independent) shoulder and hand/wrist movement called a pendulum stroke, and it's what I always tried to mimic as a player. I always wondered why it worked some days and not on other days—why I sometimes hit a power smash putt that went way beyond the hole, then left the next one well short. Now I realize what was going on: on days or stretches when I putted well, my ball position at address was precisely where it needed to be. When it was even a hair off, I struggled.

## PENDULUM PROBLEMS

When you use a pendulum stroke and your ball position is slightly off, you make contact with the handle of the club leaning away from the target or perpendicular to the ground. The result is a putt that skids and pops into the air *[sequence, below]* or is driven into the ground, depending on the ball position. So you see, the pendulum stroke provides you with only a very small window in which you can hit a solid putt with a consistent roll of the ball.

Think of it this way: a pendulum stroke is a "V," and that tiny point at the bottom of the "V" represents your chance for a solid strike on the ball with the putterface, so if your ball position is a fraction off, you miss

the putt. My Brush Stroke technique, on the other hand, removes the up-and-down-and-up arc (the "V") of the pendulum stroke, so ball position isn't as critical.

## ROTATION PROBLEMS

Some golfers actually make miniature full swings with their putters when they putt, producing face rotation and an arcing path (see previous chapter for more on this type of stroke). The incredibly gifted Ben Crenshaw was the poster boy for this method, and it does keep all aspects of the game very similar in thought, which is nice. However, using this type of stroke also leaves you susceptible to misfiring when your ball position is ever so slightly askew. It also introduces a lot of variables into your stroke that greatly increase your chances of failure.

In your full swing, the risk/reward of rotating the face of the club is necessary and manageable. A 30-yard wide fairway can fit about 642 golf balls across it, so you can very often escape unharmed when you make tiny errors. When you putt, the hole is only a little wider than two balls side by side. That's obviously a huge difference in terms of margin for error, so you can see why even the most miniscule mistake is magnified and the direction of the shot becomes much more critical.

## GLOSSARY

**PENDULUM STROKE:** A motion that involves keeping the putterface square to the intended target line from start to finish by swinging the putter straight back and then straight through. Vertical arc is introduced by the inherent shape of the pendulum, which rises on the backstroke and following contact.

**ARC STROKE:** A motion that involves opening and closing the face to the intended target line by swinging the putter to the inside on the backstroke, back to square at impact and back to the inside on the through-stroke.

**BRUSH STROKE:** A new putting motion that limits arc and face rotation, thereby decreasing the inconsistencies in contact that result from the other two stroke styles.

# ONLY ONE CHANCE AT PERFECTION

**IN A PEFECT PENDULUM** stroke the putterface must rise on the backstroke and again on the through-stroke in order to keep the pendulum motion intact. This V-shaped putter path gives you only one chance to strike the ball with the amount of loft built into your putterface—at the absolute bottom of your swing arc. If your ball position is even a hair forward of the absolute bottom, you'll strike the ball on an upswing and cause the ball to skid and jump rather than roll smoothly end over end.

**This specially marked ball shows how the ball reacts off the putterface on a mis-strike.**

**I've positioned the ball forward of where it should be. Notice how the putter is ascending into impact.**

**BIG MISTAKE** When you use a pendulum stroke, your putter will rise once you swing past the bottom of your swing arc. The only way to make perfect contact is to position the ball perfectly in your stance. This is difficult to do even for elite players.

The ball is on its way, but the ascending strike has caused it to hop instead of roll.

Not only has the poor ball position caused the ball to hop, I've imparted reverse spin.

The ball still hasn't rolled. This is the inconsistency you get when you add any arc to your stroke.

# WHY THE BRUSH STROKE IS BETTER

**MY BRUSH STROKE** is a unique putting motion that eliminates the inconsistencies that come with the standard techniques. As you follow the steps in this chapter you'll see how the Brush Stroke removes the need to swing the putter on an arc, keeps the putterhead more square to the line on the backstroke and more down the line on the through-stroke (something that doesn't happen when you swing your putter straight back and through), and makes it easy to stop the putterhead from flipping past your

**Simply put, it makes more sense to eliminate rotation in your putting stroke and to keep the putterface on the target line for as long as possible to give yourself the best chance to control the direction of the ball.** If you need a putt to travel a significant distance, you'll need some arc and possibly some face rotation in your stroke. But the closer you are to the hole, the more you want to minimize arc and face rotation. There's a greater chance for a solid strike and immediate forward roll on the ball when the handle of the club is ahead of the putterface at impact *[sequence, below]*. Studies have shown that immediate forward roll is better for controlling distance, and the stroke you learn on the following pages will teach you how to achieve that, and how to eliminate the most harmful putting errors.

**LEVEL STRIKE**
Elimating arc and face rotation by applying the principles of the Brush Stroke allow you to make square contact with the right amount of loft without having to worry too much about ball position.

> **"There's a greater chance for a solid strike when the handle is ahead of the putterface at impact."**

## ZERO ARC = PERFECT ROLL

**THE BENEFIT OF BRUSHING**
Since the Brush Stroke eliminates rotation and arc, using it allows you to contact the ball with the putterface square to your target and with the correct amount of loft. The result is an immediate forward end-over-end roll.

# REAL VS. FEEL

**THE DIFFERENCE BETWEEN** what you think you do and what you actually do when you putt is really an eye-opener. What's really crazy about it is that what you think you should do, and what you think you are doing, are both correct. Unfortunately, the cruel joke here is that you aren't really doing what you think you're doing.

Whenever I start working with a new student, I ask them what they think the relationship of the putter handle and putterface should be at impact. Most reply that the handle should be forward of the face, and at the very least, perpendicular to it at impact. Then I ask them to demonstrate their putting stroke one hand at

a time without using a putter. Inevitably they show me a flat left wrist and an angled right wrist through impact—perfect in theory and in practice. With your hands in these positions, you'll have the best results.

But here's the catch: When I take video of their strokes when they actually putt, they have an angled left wrist and a flat right wrist at impact with the handle ahead of the handle—the complete opposite of what they want to achieve and what they really thought they were achieving. This occurs because of fundamental flaws in the traditional approach to putting—mistakes you can eliminate by using a Brush Stroke.

**DO THIS!**
The most important thing you can do when putting is to keep the handle ahead (or at least even) with the face through impact—a key benefit of the Brush Stroke.

**DON'T DO THIS**
This is the putting equivalent of hari-kari—allowing your left wrist to bend and flipping the putterface past your hands. If you've ever wondered why you come up way short on one putt and jam it six feet by on the next, this is the culprit. Swinging in a pendulum fashion actually encourages this error.

# THE BRUSH STROKE SETUP

**AS I PREVIOUSLY** mentioned, the goal of the Brush Stroke is to simplify your motion by decreasing arc and rotation in your stroke. Unfortunately, you can't just jump into your old stance and make a Brush Stroke because your traditional putting grip and posture encourage rotation and arc. An object tends to swing at a right angle to whatever's holding it, and when you combine this with the facts that all putters are built with a significant lie angle and you lean your upper body forward when you putt, you're destined to create arc on both sides of the ball.

Since the goal of the Brush Stroke is to eliminate as much arc and rotation as possible, and to maneuver the putter straight back and through the impact area, you need to alter the angles in your setup so that they're more perpendicular to your target line. Follow the steps on the opposite page.

**NATURAL ARC**
The angles created by your body and putter shaft when you assume a standard putting setup add natural arc to your stroke.

**HOW FAR FORWARD SHOULD THE HANDLE BE?**
It depends on the amount of loft on your putter. The more loft, the farther forward the handle should be. I have experimented and have found that for this method, and to create immediate forward roll, 2 to 4 degrees of loft on the putter with the back of the left hand at the front of the ball at address is optimum. Maintaining this handle/putterface relationship throughout the stroke, and even increasing the lean forward through impact, will create a very nice roll.

# HOW TO ELIMINATE ARC IN YOUR SETUP

**STEP 1: GET "SITTY" WITH IT**
Forget about the posture you use at address in your full swing. When you putt feel like you're sitting with your lower body and slouching at the top of your spine. Your face should be facing directly down, not on an angle. You'll know you're doing it correctly if you feel your weight in your legs and very little pressure in your back.

**STEP 2: LOAD UP YOUR STANCE**
Put 80-90 percent of your weight on the inside of your left foot. This will shift your sternum slightly forward (important for ball positioning). To help accommodate this, widen your stance. This will stabilize your entire lower body.

**STEP 3: SET THE BALL**
Position the ball one or two inches to the left of your sternum. It's irrelevant where the ball is in relation to your feet, especially since you've widened your stance. Positioning the ball left of your sternum eliminates many of the problems ball position causes in other strokes, and forces you into a pre-set, handle-forward position with your right arm folded and ready to act as a piston when you rock your shoulders in the stroke (more on that on the following pages).

**STEP 4: GET A HEAD START**
Once you feel "sitty" and have the ball properly set, position your eyes over the ball with the top of your spine on plane with the ground. Feel like you're pushing the top of your sternum in toward your spine for more rounded shoulders. Having your shoulders "down" will keep your putter on line longer in your stroke and reduce the arc. (Bonus tip: As you walk into your putt position, put two fingers on your sternum to remind yourself to pull it in.)

**HEAD**
Facing down, with your eyes over your putt line.

**SHOULDERS**
Rounded, like you've shrugged them forward.

**BACK**
Feel like the top of your spine is parallel to the ground.

**BALL**
Positioned two inches to the left of the middle of your chest.

**WEIGHT**
Set 80 to 90 percent of it on the inside of your left foot.

# THE BRUSH STROKE GRIP

**IF YOU'VE PLAYED** for any length of time, you know how important your grip is on any shot. For the Brush Stroke, I recommend an opposing/facing palms technique with the back of your left hand and the palm of your right hand on plane and in line with the putterface. Your thumbs shouldn't be directly on top of the shaft, but rather on top with a bit of grip still showing through *[photos, opposite page]*. You should feel snug pressure between the tops of the opposing palms on the inside of the thumb pads against the grip. The pressure should be firm enough to keep you from flipping the putterhead past the handle.

The key parts of the grip are that your palms face each other and that the back of your left hand and the palm of your right hand match your face *[photos, below]*. I call this a "praying" grip, with your hands set in a typical praying position and pointing down to the ground.

**HANDS DOWN**
The trick to a good Brush Stroke grip is to bow your hands down. This hand position make is easy to eliminate rotation from your putting stroke.

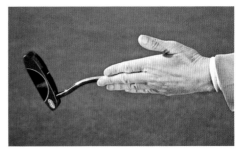

**LEFT HAND**
Feel like the back of your left hand is facing the target and opposing your right hand.

**RIGHT HAND**
Feel like your right palm is facing the target and opposing your left hand.

---

## THE BRUSH STROKE GRIP STEP-BY-STEP

**STEP 1**
Start by pressing both of your palms against the sides of the handle, with your middle fingers centered on each side of the grip and your thumbs on top. This positions the grip under your thumb pads.

**STEP 2**
Slide your left hand up and your right hand down while keeping your thumbs on top of the grip and your middle fingers on the sides of the grip. Slide your hands until the index finger on your left hand is even with the thumb on your right hand.

**STEP 3**
Without moving your thumbs, wiggle your fingers and then wrap them around the grip. If you do it correctly you should be able to hold a credit card between the bases of both of your thumbs and index fingers. You can adjust your grip from here (I like to rest my left index finger over my right ring finger). The important thing is that you create pressure between both palms, which is vital to keep you from flipping the putterhead past the handle.

**IMPORTANT: BOW YOUR WRISTS**
Did you notice when you gripped the putter from the sides and under your thumb pads how your hands were bowed downward (no wrinkles in your wrists) and the grip pointed up both forearms? This is the exact opposite of how you grip one of your irons or wedges, where you slightly cock your wrists to set the lie angle of the club when you sole it on the ground and the grip points under your forearms. The purpose of bowing your wrists in the Brush Stroke setup is to limit putterface rotation and position the putter to swing on a single plane.

> "The back of your left hand and the palm of your right hand should match your putterface."

# THE BRUSH STROKE

**ONCE YOU'VE MADE** the necessary setup adjustments, the Brush Stroke will literally "put the putter in the hole," something I often was told while learning the game and which is still great advice. And here's the wonderful part about your new stroke: the only things moving in it are your shoulders (plus a piston-like push by your right arm through impact). You simply rock them back and forth. You don't have to worry about path or face rotation. Your setup takes care of that.

Start your stroke by rocking your left shoulder down and your right shoulder up. You should feel like your right palm is facing more toward the ground at the end of your backstroke. This is important, because you want to keep that feeling through impact.

**Point the shaft at your shirt buttons to make sure you've set the ball on the target side of your forward-stroke.**

To start your forward-stroke, reverse your shoulder rock. Careful—you may feel the urge to follow the upward movement of your left shoulder and flip the putter-face up to the sky. That's a big no-no (the hole is in the ground, not the sky). The secret is to keep the angle in your right hand and wrist and try to brush the ground in front of the ball with the putterface pointing down the line, and you do this simply by straightening your right arm. Not only does this right-arm action keep the face from flipping, it keeps the handle forward through impact. This sounds a little scary because you might think "I'm going to drive the ball into the ground." That will only happen if you position the ball behind your sternum.

When you use your shoulders as your sole power source and your right arm as a piston, you eliminate the bad tendency to over-use your hands and wrists. You'll enjoy much more effective distance control as a result. And since you're minimizing rotation, you'll produce better accuracy—a great recipe for sinking putts.

## "Simply keep the angle in your right hand and wrist and try to brush the ground in front of the ball."

**ADDRESS**
Face and body down, palms opposing.

**BACKSTROKE**
Rock your
shoulders back.

**FORWARD-
STROKE**
Brush the
grass in front
of the ball.

# PUTTING IT AL TOGETHER

**WHEN YOU USE** this stroke it will feel longer going back and shorter through the ball, and this feeling will be very real and accurate. Maintaining the angle in the back of your right wrist on the through-stroke as long as possible does shorten your through-stroke. To allow for this you'll need a longer

backstroke as you eliminate the "flip." When you take the putter back a short distance, you need a lot of power and flip from your hands and wrists on the way through impact to get distance. Sometimes you get a power surge and sometimes you get a mis-hit, depending on ball position. When

you eliminate the flip of the hands and wrists as a power source, more back stroke or shoulder rocking will be necessary to have the ball travel longer distances. It will fascinate you how quickly you'll learn to judge the green speed as you strike your putts more solidly and consistently by

eliminating the flip of the wrists and hands. Your distance control will improve very quickly.

### THE PISTON
Using your right arm and elbow as a piston during the handle-forward stroke is key to a solid strike. Your right elbow should

**BACKSTROKE** You can clearly see that when I rock my shoulders back my right hand moves "on top" of my left without having to break my wrists. If you can keep this relationship intact through impact then you'll make a successful Brush Stroke.

**BACKSTROKE** The face-and-body-down setup eliminates any inside or outside movement of the putterhead—it moves straight back and then straight through.

be bent and soft into your right side at address. This is important! A high right elbow will destroy your path. On the forward-stroke, it will begin to straighten to allow you to maintain the angle in your right wrist and result in a solid strike. If your right elbow remains bent, your right wrist will start to flatten and most likely result in a "flip." The easiest way to picture the perfect strike is that you're making contact with the ball on an upstroke (since the ball is positioned in front of your sternum) but with the putterface set up for a downstroke (because the handle is in front of the putterhead).

**"It will fascinate you how quickly you'll learn to judge speed as you strike your putts more solidly by eliminating the flip of the wrists and hands."**

Right wrist remains bent all the way through.

**FORWARD-STROKE** The right elbow remains bent and, working with the shoulders, pushes the putter forward like a piston through impact.

Putt struck with perfect loft.

**FORWARD-STROKE** The putterhead "paints" the ground in front of the ball, and doesn't begin to rise until the ball is well on its way tword the cup.

# LIVE AND LEARN: SEEING IS BELIEVING

**IN MY OLD** putting posture, I would shudder at the thought of seeing an old pitch mark or spike mark on or near my line, because I knew that when I got over the ball, it was going to look like it had moved. It was so bad that I couldn't practice with a chalk line. I knew that even a chalk line wouldn't look straight to me. It was so frustrating, and it was a big part of why when I was on Tour, a "good" putting day was 28 or 29 putts.

Since I've adopted the face-down address position and Brush Stroke, I see the line of the putt in a whole new light, and now a good putting day is in the low 20s for me. If I'd only known then what I know now! With my face-down posture and my eyes over the ball, ball marks and imperfections on the green are my friends and a guide. Now when I stand behind the ball looking down the line and a ball mark is on the line I can use it as a guide. For example, if I want to start my ball at the right edge of the hole and there happens to be a ball mark or imperfection in the green just outside of the right edge, I get into my face down position and adjust the angle of my face and therefore my eyes until I see the same relationship of the hole to the ball mark that I saw from behind the ball looking down the line. Now I know when I set my putter behind the ball that I am setting it down on my chosen line.

With the techniques discussed in this chapter you'll enjoy the same sensation. Good aim—whether you're shooting skeet, pointing a water gun at a clown's mouth at an arcade or putting—starts with setting your eyes down your target line.

## "If your putter is too long— which it probably is—you're really hurting yourself."

**EYE LINE**
The face-down posture of the Brush Stroke allows you to see the line in your setup the same way you saw it when you were making your read because it gives you the exact same perspective.

# LAST STEPS: DETERMINING EYE ALIGNMENT AND PUTTER LENGTH

NO!

A marker will look different from your initial read when you look at it using standard posture.

YES!

Any line you see from your putt-read stance will replicate itself when you view it from a face-down setup.

**LENGTH ISSUES**
My old putter was much longer than the one I currently use with my Brush Stroke. The longer length naturally created too many angles at address, and increased rotation both back and through—not good.

**TAKE THE TEST**
Take your Brush Stroke stance with your current putter, and slide your hands down the shaft until they're in the correct position. Where they end up is the correct length for you (notice how much shorter my putter needs to be for the Brush Stroke compared to my old putter).

**PLACE A BALL** 15 feet from a hole. Tee up another ball on the green just to the right or left of your intended line about three or four feet from the hole. Now, from behind the ball, look with both eyes and confirm that you have placed the teed ball just off of your intended line. With your current putter, set up to the ball and turn your head to look down your line at the hole. Has the teed ball moved? Do you want to aim more right or left of the ball? If the teed ball looks like it has certainly moved (and I bet it does), adjust your posture to get into a face down instead of an angled/face up position. Rotate your head (moving your chin under, not across) toward the hole and shuttle your hands up or down the length of your current putter while adjusting your putterface angle and posture until the teed ball is in the same place it was when you were standing behind your intended line. Don't be surprised if you're

near the very bottom of the putter grip. I was putting with a 34.5" putter in my old posture and now I use a 31" putter in the posture where I can see the line properly.

This test is important. When you use a putter that's too long, you have to take up the slack of the length by flattening the lie angle. This causes you to have an angle in the top of your wrist near your thumbs and the putter under the heel pad of your hand. Your grip probably resembles a full-swing grip, and is positioned to allow rotation to creep into your stroke (not a good thing). The other compensation for a putter that's too long is to bend your elbows outward instead of inward, a move that puts an angle in both of your wrists and adds loft on the putter at impact (also not a good thing). In short, if your putter is too long—which it probably is—you're really hurting yourself, so check it out and get the proper length.

# 6

# Read Greens
# Like a Pro

For many, green-reading is part mystery and part luck—a slope and speed crapshoot. Those who are good at it learned through years of trial and error. But that's no longer the case, as technology has sped up the learning curve at a lightning-fast pace. Now anyone can read greens like a veteran in seconds flat.

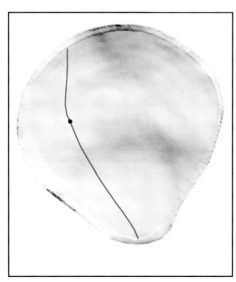

# The Green Machine
# Mark Sweeney

*Founder, AimPoint Technologies, Orlando, Fla.*

The man behind the technology that accurately predicts the roll of any putt—the AimPoint graphics you see on televised golf broadcasts—takes green-reading one step further by placing the technology in the palm of your hands. With Mark Sweeney's help, finding the right line is easy.

**W**HAT IF, instead of relying solely on touch and feel and mere guesstimates of the proper line, golfers could use physics and geometry to correctly read every putt within 20 feet? It seems like a stretch, but technology like this is already being used on all professional tours.

I call this advancement predictive-putt technology. By modeling greens with sophisticated laser-scanning programs and applying formulas that account for everything from gravity and green speed to slope and momentum, I helped develop a system that accurately predicts how any putt will roll across any portion of any green. (You might have seen my technology at work in Golf Channel's PGA Tour coverage.) That data allowed me to design "Aim Charts®" that tell you precisely how far inside or outside the hole you need to aim to drain every putt within 20 feet of the hole.

It's not magic, it's science—and don't worry, it's not as complicated as it sounds. To remove the guessing game from putting, you simply need to identify the Zero Line on the green, an imaginary boundary that acts like a road map to better green-reading: putts on the right side of a green's Zero Line will always break from right to left, while putts on the left side will break left to right. The further you are from the line, the harder the putt will break. Piece of cake. Here's how to put the technology to work for you.

**5 Things I'll Teach You In This Chapter**

**1** How to find the Zero Line—the common link to reading putts on all greens.

**2** How to use the Zero Line in your reads for foolproof results.

**3** Unique characteristics of common green shapes to take the mystery out of slope.

**4** A pre-putt green-reading routine you can count on every time.

**5** How to pinpoint your aim using our proprietary Aim Charts®.

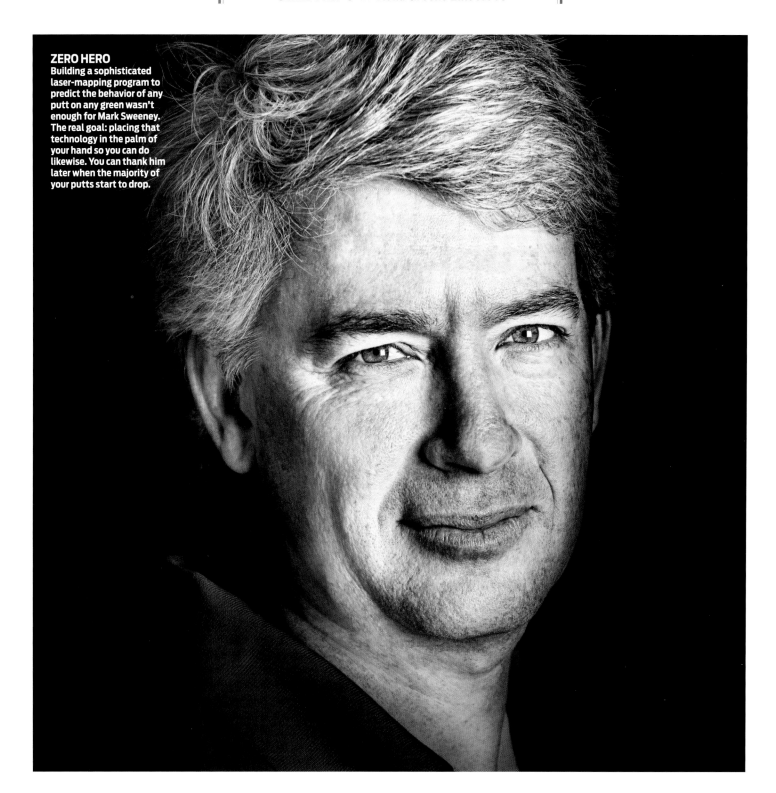

**ZERO HERO**
Building a sophisticated laser-mapping program to predict the behavior of any putt on any green wasn't enough for Mark Sweeney. The real goal: placing that technology in the palm of your hand so you can do likewise. You can thank him later when the majority of your putts start to drop.

## ALL ABOUT ME

**Name:** Mark Sweeney

**Teaching since:** 2007

**Where you can find me:** AimPoint Technologies, Orlando, Fla.

**Where I've played:** I am an amateur golfer constantly in search of lower scores, just like you

**Who I've instructed:** Padraig Harrington, Scott McCarron, Charlie Wi, Bobby Clampett, Bo Van Pelt and Peter Jacobsen, among others. I have also instructed the Tour caddies for Y.E. Yang and JB Holmes

**Awards I've won:** The 29th annual Sports Emmy® Award for Technical Achievement (2007)

**My best contribution to the game:** Developing the AimPoint Putting Line seen on Golf Channel telecasts since 2007, and a systematic way to apply this technology to help players read greens across all skill levels, from Tour professional to recreational novice

**For more instruction:** golf.com/ bestputtingbook aimpointgolf.com

# "There are multiple points on any green from which the ball will roll straight—a perfect balance between left and right."

**T**O MOST GOLFERS, greens are a confusing series of humps, rises, valleys and curves—a maddening arrangement of three-dimensional shapes that the mind can't possibly compute without the help of a Harvard physics degree. The undulating nature of most greens is an architect's final defense—one final challenge in a series of many as you traverse every hole from the tee to the cup. It's also what gives greens their beauty and aesthetic appeal. Yes, it would be a lot easier to score if every green were as flat as a piece of paper, but, let's face it, they wouldn't look as nice and there's no doubt players are partly drawn to the game for the look and feel of different venues—the inherent art in the courses we play.

The point is, slope isn't going anywhere anytime soon, and if you don't learn how to analyze it, you won't have much chance of improving your scores. The green-reading X-factor for most players has always been slope. Speed—anyone can tell the difference between fast and slow in just a few putts. And grain can be judge by most experienced golfers in seconds. Slope, as you're aware, can be an entirely different story.

I'm an active recreational player just like you who, in the past, shared many of the same doubts about green-reading due to the intricacies of slope. As part of the team that developed the technology to map greens and expose the way putts behave on them with advanced laser technology (the AimPoint graphics you see on golf telecasts), I quickly learned that, despite all of the curves, rises and bends, greens are fairly simple shapes. You just have to know how to break them down.

The trick is to understand that you really only have to worry about the area close to the hole, not the entire green (although, as you'll learn, the overall shape of a green has a lot to do with how putts break, but again, it's not as complicated as you're making it out to be). The other critical key is to come to grips with the fact that, like all things in the universe, greens like to achieve a certain balance—a symmetry and a harmony. For putting purposes, the balance exists in terms of left and right, and up and down. I don't care how crazy a green looks, there are multiple points on its surface from which you can aim dead straight at the hole—a perfect balance between left and right break. And this happens for every possible pin location on every green ever constructed.

Knowing that this left/right balance exists—and then being able to locate its center for the particular putt you're facing—is the secret to demystifying slope and its effect on the ball's roll. It's also the foundation of my green-reading technique based on the information we've gathered by applying AimPoint technology to hundreds of greens on the PGA Tour. Its name: the Zero Line. Here's all you need to know: putts to the right of the Zero Line break left, and putts to the left of the Zero Line break right. This is the green-reading magic bullet most golfers have been missing.

To make matters even easier, I've developed simple-to-read charts that show you just how much left or right most putts break in relation to the Zero Line for given distances and green speeds—an atlas of aim points for every putt you'll ever face in your golfing life. Your lone job is to find the Zero Line, and apply a few simple adaptations of it based on three very common green shapes. Then, holing more putts is simply aiming correctly and hitting the putt with the right speed.

## WATCH & LEARN

When you see this icon, go to **golf.com/bestputtingbook** for a free video lesson with green-reading expert Mark Sweeney.

**ONE LINE FITS ALL**
There's a Zero Line for every putt you'll face, turning a vast majority of your reads into a simple assessment of left or right and up or down. Its existence also means that if you can read one putt, you can read them all.

PUTT PATH

ZERO LINE

# THE ZERO LINE

**HERE'S A BOLD STATEMENT:** The Zero Line is the most important green-reading discovery in decades. I truly believe that, because it influences every putt. Extending from one side of the green through the hole to the other side of the green, the Zero Line represents every possible putt on a given green for which the net break is zero (the "perfect balance" I mentioned on the previous pages). For example, a putt from the Zero Line that breaks three feet to the left would at some point on its path to the hole also have to break three feet to the right, for a net break of zero. That means that the aiming point for any putt from the Zero Line is the heart of the hole, regardless of whether or not the putt is straight.

## AN EASY IMAGE

The quickest way to come to grasp with the Zero Line is to think of a perfectly flat putting surface with a hole cut in the dead center. Since there isn't any slope to this surface, there are an infinite number of Zero Lines—every putt is a straight putt. Now, imagine lifting the rear of this putting green to create a straight back-to-front slope *[graphic, right]*. Suddenly, those infinite number of Zero Lines boil down to a single one for each possible hole position: a straight line that runs from the back of the green through the cup and through the front of the green. Any putt off this line will feature some amount of break.

Of course, most greens are tilted like this, but also feature high points, low points, tiers, etc. Nonetheless, the Zero Line rule applies, it's just that it becomes more of a curved line instead of straight, but it always runs from near the high point above the hole, across the hole, and to near the lowest point below the hole.

When most golfers start learning about the Zero Line, they often struggle because they try to draw it across the entire green. As you'll learn later in this chapter, this can be difficult, especially when you start analyzing complex greens. The secret is that you only need to worry about what the Zero Line is doing near the cup, say within 20 feet, because your goal isn't to sink more 30-footers. Your goal is to make more of the mid-range and short putts you've been missing due to bad reads. Limiting your comprehension of the Zero Line to the area around the hole makes the process simple and infinitely easier to comprehend. Our laser-mapping system can trace the Zero Line across any green in milliseconds. Once you become comfortable with the system, you'll be able to do likewise.

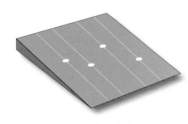

> **"You only need to worry what the Zero Line does relative to your putt."**

**GREEN-READING MADE EASY**
An easy way to grasp the Zero Line is that it's the line for which the net break of any putt is zero, which means it could be a straight putt or one which breaks left and right in equal amounts. When your ball is on the Zero Line, all you have to do is aim at the cup no matter the distance of the putt. The ball will always end up where you've aimed: the hole.

ZERO LINE

AIM LINE

**ZERO LINE 101**
The correct aim
for all putts that
originate on the
Zero Line is straight
at the cup. If the
putt breaks, it will
break in at least
two directions to
create a net break
of zero.

# THE POWER OF THE ZERO LINE

**WHY DOES THE** Zero Line matter, and how exactly does it affect your putt's roll? Here's all you need to know:

**Rule 1.** **All putts originating to the left of the Zero Line will break left to right. All those originating to the right will break right to left.**

That's groundbreaking stuff for your green-reading skills! Once you're able to identify Zero Lines, you'll never again need to agonize over which direction a putt will break. You'll only have to worry about the speed of your putts and how much break to play.

**Rule 2.** **The amount a putt will break increases as its distance from the Zero Line increases.**

Which of course also means putts near the Zero Line will require you to play less break. This holds true on all greens, whether they're slightly pitched or wildly undulating.

**Rule 3.** **For a given radius around a hole, a putt will tend to break most aggressively from the "2:30" and "9:30" positions relative to the Zero Line.**

Imagine a clock. If the "upper" Zero Line is 12 o'clock, the "lower" Zero Line will generally lay somewhere between 5 o'clock and 7 o'clock. For green speeds around 10, the 2:30 and 9:30 maximum break points apply; for green speeds 8 or slower, the maximum break points will decrease toward 3:00 and 9:00. As you raise the green speed to 12 and beyond, the maximum break points increase toward the 2:00 and 10:00 positions. Still, in most cases we are talking about a difference of an inch or less of break, so don't spend too much time sweating the details. (This concept is most effective for putts inside of 20 feet because beyond that range the surface of the green starts to show more variation in grade percentage and direction of the slope.)

## IT WORKS!

The first time I tested the Zero Line on a course I made 6 out of 8 putts from outside of 10 feet. That's a hit rate of 75 percent from a range where Tour pros struggle to covert 25 percent of their putts. And every time I play now I drain a couple of 20-foot putts, which used to be a rarity. Not only has this method reinvigorated my love for the short game, it has eliminated any sense of anxiety or nervousness that I used to have on all putts outside of 3 feet. PGA Tour veteran Scott McCarron tried my system after a putting slump in 2008 left him 164th in total putting. Less than a year later he had vaulted to 14th in that category.

> "Putts nearer the Zero Line require you to play less break."

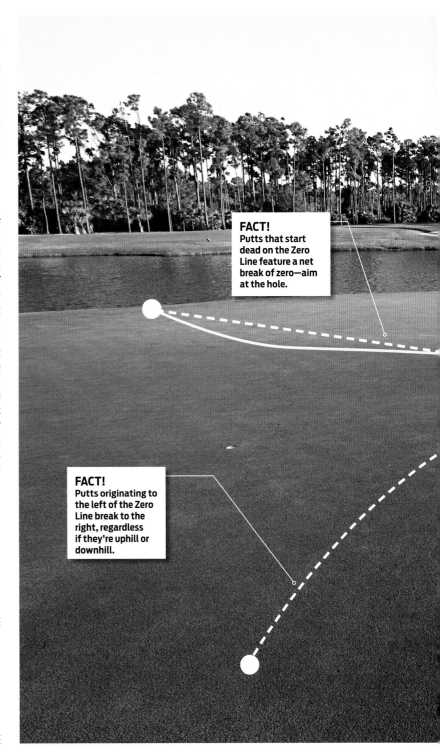

**FACT!** Putts that start dead on the Zero Line feature a net break of zero—aim at the hole.

**FACT!** Putts originating to the left of the Zero Line break to the right, regardless if they're uphill or downhill.

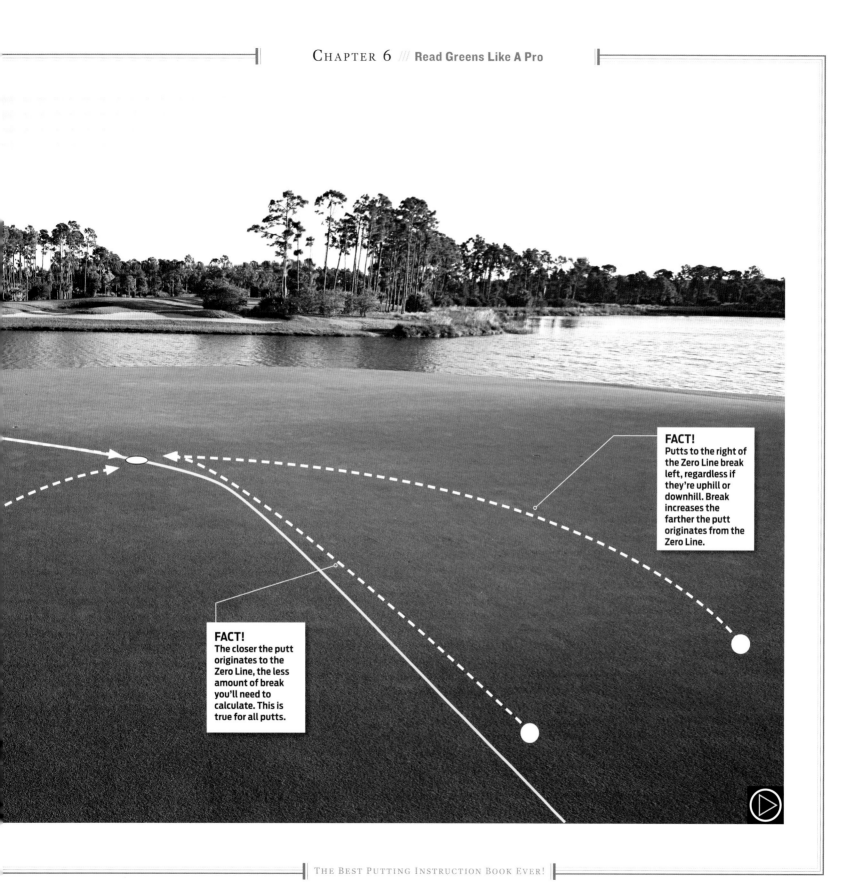

**FACT!**
Putts to the right of the Zero Line break left, regardless if they're uphill or downhill. Break increases the farther the putt originates from the Zero Line.

**FACT!**
The closer the putt originates to the Zero Line, the less amount of break you'll need to calculate. This is true for all putts.

# FINDING THE ZERO LINE: **PRACTICE**

**HEAD OUT TO** the practice putting green and find a 12-foot putt that features a noticeable degree of slope. As you survey this putt, eyeball the highest point above the hole and the lowest point below the hole, and draw in your mind's eye a line connecting the two that also runs through the cup. Keep in mind that the vast majority of time this line will feature some curve unless the high and low points you pinpointed are on exact opposite sides of the cup. Now, go to your high point and roll some balls (like a miniature bowling motion) toward the hole. If the balls go in, you nailed the high spot. If they trail off to the left, then move to your right, and roll the balls again. Keep doing this until you can nail the Zero Line from both sides of the cup.

This is great practice, and actually is the way I demonstrate the Zero Line in my clinics.

## APPLYING WHAT YOU LEARNED

Now, stand on the Zero Line on the low side of the hole (again, you can roll balls toward the cup to double-check your estimate). As you stand there, come to grips with Rule #1 on the previous pages: any putt to your right will break left, and any putt on your left will break right. This holds true if you're standing on the Zero Line above the hole, too. This point isn't simple advice, a hunch or a feeling—it's a cold-hard fact that basically breaks the multitude of rolls into 4 simple paths: 1) uphill left-to-right, 2) uphill right-to-left, 3) downhill

right-to-left, and 4) downhill left-to-right. The amount of break depends on how far the ball sits from the Zero Lines. As stated in Rule #2 on the previous pages, the farther the ball sits from the Zero Line, the more it will break (the exact amount we'll discuss in just a few pages).

## BREAKING POINTS

The underlying geometry of putting remains the same whether you have a putt from 5 feet or 15 feet, and whether the green speed is 8 or 12. We can use this information to give us a reliable starting point for reading a putt. The table at right shows the expected break amounts for 10-foot putts on a "planar" green Stimping at 8 and sloped at 2 percent grade (the most common situation you'll

see from 10 feet). Notice that the break amounts are symmetrical on either side of the clock face and that the biggest break happens at 2:30 and 9:30.

**BREAK AMOUNTS**
*(10-ft Putt, 2% Grade, 8 Stimp)*

| Position | Break | Position | Break |
|----------|-------|----------|-------|
| 12:00 | 0" | 6:00 | 0" |
| 12:30 | 3" | 11:30 | 3" |
| 1:00 | 5" | 11:00 | 5" |
| 1:30 | 7" | 10:30 | 7" |
| 2:00 | 8" | 10:00 | 8" |
| 2:30 | 9" | 9:30 | 9" |
| 3:00 | 8" | 9:00 | 8" |
| 3:30 | 7" | 8:30 | 7" |
| 4:00 | 6" | 8:00 | 6" |
| 4:30 | 5" | 7:30 | 5" |
| 5:00 | 3" | 7:00 | 3" |
| 5:30 | 2" | 6:30 | 2" |

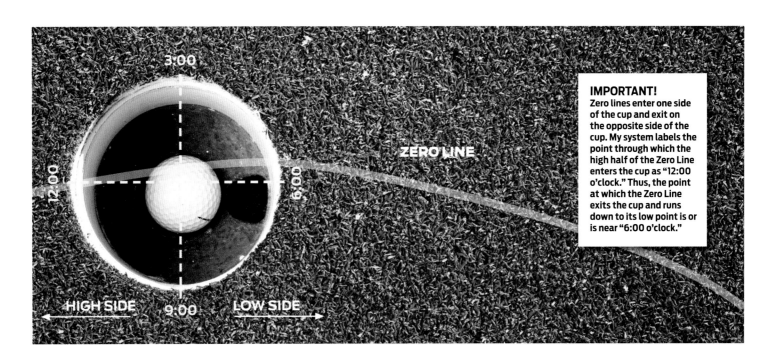

**IMPORTANT!**
Zero lines enter one side of the cup and exit on the opposite side of the cup. My system labels the point through which the high half of the Zero Line enters the cup as "12:00 o'clock." Thus, the point at which the Zero Line exits the cup and runs down to its low point is or is near "6:00 o'clock."

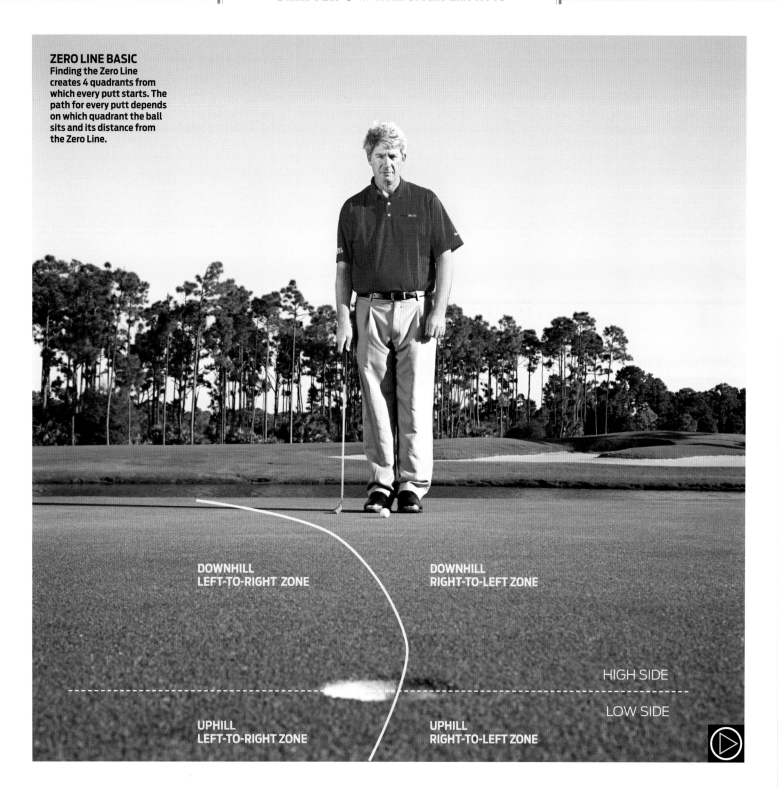

**ZERO LINE BASIC**
Finding the Zero Line creates 4 quadrants from which every putt starts. The path for every putt depends on which quadrant the ball sits and its distance from the Zero Line.

DOWNHILL
LEFT-TO-RIGHT ZONE

DOWNHILL
RIGHT-TO-LEFT ZONE

HIGH SIDE

LOW SIDE

UPHILL
LEFT-TO-RIGHT ZONE

UPHILL
RIGHT-TO-LEFT ZONE

# FINDING THE ZERO LINE: ON THE COURSE

**LOCATING ZERO LINES**, or your "12:00" and "6:00" positions around the hole, can take practice. But with a little experience and know-how you'll have no trouble identifying them. The best way to estimate where the line runs for putts inside of 15 feet is to try and feel the inflection point under your feet where a downslope becomes an upslope, or vice versa. Focus on the three to five steps in the vicinity of the inflection point *[photo, below]*. Sometimes it is a sharp crest, which you feel from one step to the next, and sometimes it

happens gradually over two or three steps. If it happens gradually, pick the center point. Now you have the primary reference point for reading your putt.

Some holes are cut on extremely flat areas of the green, sometimes on less than a 1 percent grade. So you may have a hard time seeing the slope and feeling the inflection. In that case, try to determine the highest point above the hole and walk to that spot. Imagine that you have a hose and you're streaming water in the direction of the hole. The water will fun-

nel toward the hole and follow a certain line as is it drains off the green. That, roughly, is the Zero Line.

After you have developed the ability to feel the inflection point, a quick and easy method of doing so during play is make it a part of your routine while walking on the green to mark your ball. Instead of walking directly to your ball, take a circuitous path to it that passes over the inflection point. You'll notice it almost immediately as long as the slope grade is at least 1.5 percent.

**STEP 1**
Walk back and forth around where you think the Zero Line exists either below or above the hole (depending on which side the ball sits) and use your feet to feel the inflection point: the point where downwhill becomes uphill and vice-versa)

MY FEET SENSE A CHANGE IN SLOPE—THE INFLECTION POINT—ABOUT HERE

"Try to feel the inflection point under your feet where a downslope becomes an upslope, and vice versa."

**STEP 2**
Once your feet have told you were the slope changes direction you've nailed the Zero Line. With this all-important reference, you can now asses the break of your putt by its location and its distance from the Zero Line.

THIS BALL IS BREAKING RIGHT TO LEFT BASED ON ITS POSITION RELATIVE TO THE ZERO LINE.

SENSED INFLECTION POINT

# ZERO LINES AND COMMON GREEN SHAPES

## GREEN TYPE 1: PLANAR

**JUST AS THERE** are three primary colors (red, yellow, and blue), there are also three primary shapes that you will find within 20 feet of the hole on almost every green: planar, saddle, and crown. (Were you expecting squares, triangles, and octagons?) Knowing these three shapes is critical because every green's surface is comprised of one, two, or all three of these shapes, and they all influence how your ball rolls.

**A PLANAR** section of a green has one high side and one low side, and the surface slopes evenly in the same direction. Think of a wedge. The majority of all pin positions you play will be on planar levels, and they are by far the easiest kinds of putts to read.

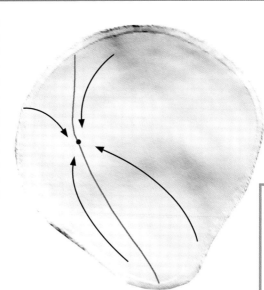

**ONE ZERO**
Since there is only one high side and one low side on a planar green, there is only one Zero Line for each hole location.

**PLANAR EXAMPLE**
The 18th at East Lake C.C. in Atlanta, host of the TOUR Championship, features a classic planar green.

**SIMPLE**
Think of a wedge.

# GREEN TYPE 2: SADDLES

**A SADDLE** is a concave section of a green created in the low area between two shoulders. Some architects, including Pete Dye, will design greens with multiple saddles created by multiple shoulders. The trick to saddles is that there are two Zero Lines—one runs through the center of the saddle and the other runs between the high points. Zero Lines typically run 12:00 to 6:00 and 10:00 to 2:00.

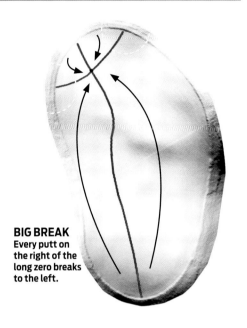

**BIG BREAK**
Every putt on the right of the long zero breaks to the left.

**CONCAVE**
Picture a valley between two ranges.

**SADDLE EXAMPLE**
The South Course at Dove Mountain (Tucson, Ariz) features a wicked saddle on No. 15.

# GREEN TYPE 3: CROWNS

**A CROWN** is a convex area of the green, the center of which is a high point where the green slopes downward in opposite directions on either side. Crowns are notoriously difficult to read because they appear so flat to the eye that most people miss them altogether, especially when the "crowning" is subtle. Like a saddle, a crown creates two Zero Line. The second one, in this case, runs across the ridge on the crown.

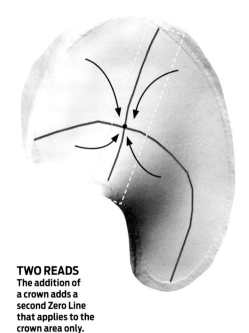

**TWO READS**
The addition of a crown adds a second Zero Line that applies to the crown area only.

**CONCAVE**
Picture a contact lens.

**CROWN EXAMPLE**
The 14th green at Pebble Beach G.L. features a notieable crown. The front-side drop-off is very severe.

# HOW TO USE ZERO LINES TO HOLE MORE PUTTS

**ONCE YOU HAVE** identified the Zero Line, stand on it and eyeball where your ball is relative to the line. Although my system allows you to simplify the read process and gives you an idea of the kind of break to expect, you still need to nail the exact amount of break. That's why we develop Aim Charts® that tell you where to aim for every putt you'll ever face using the data from our laser-mapping program that predicts the roll of all putts using a complex math formula and a wicked piece of software. Your job, then, is to simply check the ball's position and then refer to the appropriate chart for your green speed to quickly calculate how much break you need to play.

## INSTANT CADDY

The Aim Charts are ultra-specific. They'll tell you, for example, that if your ball is at the 7:00 position 15 feet away from the cup on a green Stimping at 10, you'll need to aim your putt three inches left of the hole *[see Aim Chart®, opposite page].* If your putt is at 1:00 at the same distance and on the same green, then it will break about 10 inches right to left. If the slope around the hole seems severe (more than 3 percent), then simply switch to the appropriate Aim Chart®. There are individual charts that compute slopes from 1 to 4 percent.

If referring to a chart before every 10-footer sounds laborious, don't sweat it. You'll quickly realize that you only need to learn four expected break amounts per distance, because 12:00 and 6:00 have zero net break, 2:00 and 3:00 have the same break (at recreational green speeds), and the positions mirror each other across the clock face—so 1:00 is the same as 11:00, 2:00 is the same as 10:00, etc.

You will also realize it is unnecessary to memorize the actual break amount because you will start instinctively looking at the correct aim point depending on your distance and angle to the hole. The goal—and you should work on this on the practice green—is to quickly train your intuition about how much a putt should break based on your growing awareness of where the Zero Line is.

In addition to seeing how the break increases and decreases with predictability, you will quickly discover the difference in speed between uphill and downhill putts. In fact, you might ram your first several downhill putts past the hole until you get a feel for how much softer you have to hit downhill putts vs. uphill putts from the same distance. You'll also notice that your downhill putts that miss will be spread in a much wider grouping than your uphill putts that miss. That's because downhill putts are much more sensitive to aim and speed errors than uphill putts, particularly downhill putts from the Maximum Break Points. The moral of the story: try to leave yourself uphill putts and avoid the Maximum Break Points!

With some advanced training under the watchful eye of an Aim-Point Certified Instructor, your Aim Charts® can help you read any putt on any green.

"Your job, then, is to simply check the ball's position and then refer to the appropriate chart."

**AIM CHART®**
**Stimp 8**
*Aim (inches) from edge of hole*

12:00 · 11:00 · 1:00 · 10:00 · 2:00 · 9:00 · 3:00 · 8:00 · 4:00 · 7:00 · 5:00 · 6:00

20' · 15' · 10' · 5'

3 · 3 · 6 · 6 · 6 · Avg. (2.0%) · 6 · 4 · 4 · 1 · 1

5' · 10' · 15' · 20'

## HOW TO READ THIS CHART

Imagine you've stuck your approach to 10 feet right of the hole. If you've identified the Zero Line and know for sure that the putt will break right to left and that you're located at, say, the 4 o'clock position, you now know precisely where to aim: 4 inches right of the cup. With an assist from physics, you have eliminated many potentially misleading ideas about how your 10-footer might behave.

**CHECK IT:** There are multiple charts to account for various distances, green slope severity and green speeds (I've only listed the breaks for 10-foot putts here, but each chart lists breaks for all putts up to 20 feet. Use this example as a guide. If you're interested in obtaining an Aim Chart® for every putt you'll ever face, book a lesson with a certified AimPoint instructor, or search the app store for your favorite smart phone, or visit www.aimpointgolf.com.

# 7

# How to Aim at the Right Spot

Are you a linear putter or a nonlinear putter? What's the difference? The answers to these questions turn merely good putters into great ones—they're the final pieces of your putting puzzle that make consistently rolling the ball into the hole easy.

# The Aiming Expert
# Mike Shannon

*Putting Instructor, Sea Island Golf Learning Center, Sea Island, Ga.*

The world's foremost authority on linear and nonlinear putting shows you the correct way to aim your putts according to what you see, a technique that will allow you to get more of them in the hole without changing your stroke

**I'VE TAUGHT** a lot of players—dozens of Tour professionals and thousands of amateurs—over the years, and I've watched them spend countless, sometimes agonizing hours trying to perfect their putting stokes and overall technique. While I applaud these players' dedication and work ethic, simply logging time on the practice green grooving mechanics until they're as solid as possible usually doesn't get the job done. All it does is provide you with the *potential* to become a great putter. The players who are able to make the leap to greatness are the ones who learn how to forget mechanics and focus more on the absolute end goal of putting—rolling that little white ball into the hole. And that starts with aim.

Good green reading, top-of-the-line gear and a solid stroke don't mean a darn thing unless you aim your putter correctly, and correct aim goes beyond just pointing the putterface in the direction you want the ball to start. Your aim needs to match how your eyes interpret the line, not the line itself. Some players see every line as straight; others tend to work in curves. They're either linear putters (straight-line viewers) or nonlinear putters (curved-line viewers), and if you don't take your natural view tendencies into account when you address the ball and aim your putter, you have almost zero chance of making the putt. You'll play too much break or not enough almost every time. You'll putt with a feeling of conflict—not a good mind-set when you're facing a long lag or a tricky three-footer. But if you learn to cater to your mind's eye, the putts will start to fall in droves, as if by magic.

**5 Things I'll Teach You In This Chapter**

**1** How to take advantage of your eyes' natural aiming abilities.

**2** Discover how your mind reads putts— either as straight lines or curves.

**3** Determine how much you're misaiming your putter.

**4** Establish a pre-putt routine that allows you to see lines clearly.

**5** Fine-tune your green reading to match your natural aim tendencies.

**THE EYES HAVE IT**
Mike Shannon's research
on line perception has
helped dozens of PGA Tour
professionals take the
guesswork out of aim. With
his advice you'll discover if you
see lines as curved or straight,
and how to adjust your aim
to take advantage of your
natural sight tendencies.

## "A player is born either linear or nonlinear. You can't be both, and you can't choose which kind you want to be."

**O**VER 92 PERCENT of all the putts you'll face in your golfing lifetime will feature some amount of break. That's quite a majority, so it makes sense that the better you become at reading and executing breaking putts the better your scores will be.

Breaking putts are much different than straight ones, and in more important ways than just the addition of left or right slope. Everyone sees straight putts as straight. My research shows that some players see curved putts as straight, too, while others see them as curved. This means that there are two distinct kinds of players. There are feel (right-brain) players who like to deal in curves, and there are analytical (left-brain) players who like to break down everything they see into straight lines.

Here's what I mean: Imagine you're in the middle of the fairway facing a mid-iron approach. During your pre-shot routine you look at your target and draw a picture in your mind's eye of the type of shot you want to hit—high and straight, high draw, whatever. If the shot happens to be a high draw, an analytical player will visualize this shot as being straight, even though they're planning a right-to-left curve. A feel player sees and visualizes the curve.

The same thing happens on the green when you read some break into your putt. Even though both kinds of players see the putt as breaking, an analytical player will interpret it as straight and aim to a point—usually the high point of the break—to make this putt as linear as possible. That's why I call them linear putters. Once a linear putter has his spot, all he's interested in is rolling the ball to that spot and letting gravity do the rest. To a linear putter, every putt is straight.

On the other hand, feel players focus on the curve and the perceived shape of the putt. They're not interested in lines. They're nonlinear. They see the ball curving into the cup, not traveling in a straight line to a certain spot. In fact, they lack the ability to aim at a spot without feeling a certain amount of angst or conflict. If you tell a nonlinear player to aim four inches to the right of the cup, they'll aim eight inches to the right of the cup. When their putt comes to rest, it will stop four inches to the right of the cup. The reason for this is that a nonlinear putter doesn't view the four-inch spot as the start of the putt, like a linear putter does. A nonlinear putter sees the four-inch spot as the end.

What we're talking about is a player's basic personality characteristics. A player is born either linear or nonlinear. You can't be both. You can't choose which kind you want to be, and you can't change from one to another. As we go through life, we all acquire certain personality characteristics based on our environment or profession. The most successful athletes (putters, as it pertains to this book) are those who perform in sync with their basic personality characteristics. The most frustrated are those who try to incorporate their acquired personality characteristics. In other words, you can't fake success.

## GLOSSARY

**Linear Putter**
Makes every putt a straight putt by aiming at a spot.

**Nonlinear Putter**
Deals in curves and sees the cup as the target.

## WATCH & LEARN

 When you see this icon go to to **golf.com/bestputtingbook** for a free video lesson with aiming guru Mike Shannon.

**RECONCILABLE DIFFERENCES**
The secret to holing more putts is to match your aiming style to your personality. Players who see things in curves (nonlinear) should focus on the hole. Linear putters are better off aiming at a spot along the break, which turns any breaking putt into a straight one.

LINEAR TARGET

NONLINEAR TARGET

# FINDING YOUR PUTT PERSONALITY MATCH

**THE BEST PUTTERS** in the world match their putting styles to their personalities. In other words, analytical players apply linear putting techniques, and feel players apply nonlinear putting techniques. Unfortunately, the majority of recreational players are caught somewhere in between because 1) they don't know if they have a feel or analytical personality and, 2) they use both methods on different days and on different greens during the same round. As a result, most players putt in conflict—a conflict between their sense of sight (which is linear) and their sense of touch and feel (which is nonlinear). The more conflict a player experiences when he stands over a putt, the less likely the ball will find the bottom of the cup, even if his stroke is fundamentally perfect. Step 1 to resolving this conflict is to ask yourself: "Am I an analytical player or a feel player?"

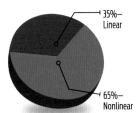

35%— Linear

65%— Nonlinear

**Most of the population is nonlinear; on the PGA Tour the discrepancy is even larger (85% nonlinear to 15% linear).**

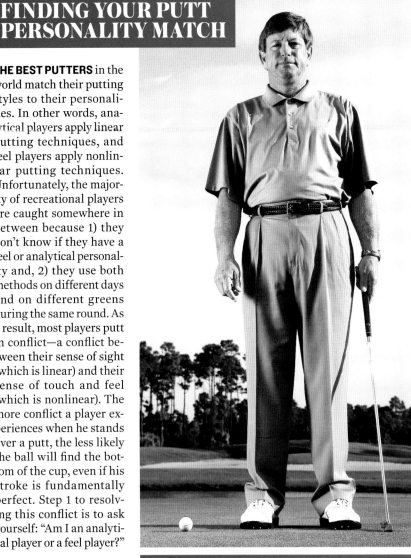

**TRAIT TALK**
Your linear or nonlinear personality permeates everything you do, not just the way you putt.

## YOU'RE AN ANALYTICAL/LINEAR PUTTER IF...

- You have a tendency to be bound by structure and routine.
- You like to arrive at the golf course at the same time before you tee off.
- In the locker room, you dress and put your shoes on in the same order every time.
- On the practice tee you hit the same number of balls with the same clubs.
- You prefer to play the same course, over and over, rather than seeking out new venues.

## YOU'RE A FEEL/NONLINEAR PUTTER IF...

- You don't like to be bound by structure or routine.
- You never arrive at the course at the same time—some days you're there an hour and a half before your tee time, and other days you're rushing from the car to the first tee without a minute to spare.
- Your pre-round routine is varied. You may go to the locker room to change your spikes or you might just lace them on in the parking lot. Some days you go through a bucket to get warm and on others you only hit 15 balls before you feel like you're ready to play.
- You're eager to play whenever, wherever, even at a moment's notice.

# TAKE THE TEST

**THE PERSONALITY TRAITS** at left should give you some good clues about your putting tendencies. To truly determine if you're a linear or nonlinear putter, try my aim test.

For this test you'll need a laser that you can attach to your putterhead (you can pick one up at your local golf shop) and a small 2 x 4 with a circle drawn on it to mimic the width of a cup. Find a straight 10-foot putt on the practice green, place the 2 x 4 on the ground behind the hole with the circle facing you and aim your putterhead at the circle using the laser as your guide. If you have trouble aiming correctly, try moving the ball back or forward in your stance. Once you've nailed your aim on this straight putt, find a curving putt (about 6 to 12 inches of break) of the same length. Read the break, and then position the circle on the board to your new start line *[photo, right]*. Now, go through the rest of your pre-putt routine, settle into your stance and aim your putterface at the circle. Where is the laser pointing?

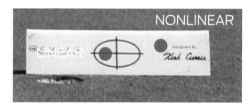
NONLINEAR

Linear putters are more likely to repeat their straight-putt aim on curved putts than nonlinear putters.

**If the laser points at the circle or close to it, you're a linear putter.** You've computed this curving putt as a straight line, and aimed your putter as accurately as you did on the straight putt.

**If the laser points outside the circle on the high side of the putt, you're a nonlinear putter.** You've added curve to this already curving putt because you don't like straight lines. Usually, a nonlinear putter will point the laser as far away from the circle as they've read the break. (i.e., if you read three inches of break, your laser likely missed the circle by three inches).

**AIM GAME**
A laser and a 2 x 4 tell you for sure whether you see putts as linear or nonlinear.

LINEAR TARGET

**LINEAR MUST**
Aim the putter with
your eyes at a spot
along the break to
turn any curved putt
into a straight one.

# LINEAR PUTTING

### THE BASICS
Straight lines are a linear putter's best friend.
Everything a linear putter does on the greens
is devoid of curves, so if you've tested positive
for linearity on the previous page, it's important that you create as many straight lines as
possible, and this starts with your aim. Even
though you know the putt is going to curve,
aim at a spot along the break and make the
stroke you need to get the ball to that point.
This turns a breaking putt into a straight one,
and this should feel natural to you. Use an
intermediate spot to complete your aim.

### SOME EXTRA HELP
To appease your straight-line preference,
choose a putter that has a lot of straight lines
in its design—look for square heads, aiming
marks and avoid large, curved mallets. It's also

a good idea to draw a
line on your ball and
aim the line (or the
ball's logo) at your spot.
You're looking for as
much help as possible
to aim your putterface
at your spot.

**A putter with a lot of
straight lines [below] is
a better tool for linear
putting than one with
curves [right].**

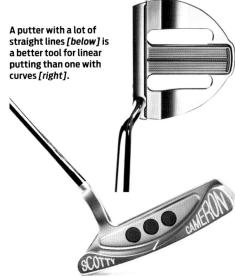

# NONLINEAR PUTTING

## THE BASICS

If you tested out as a nonlinear putter, then you need to learn how to tap into your acute sense of touch and feel and start to really see things the way you want to see them—in curves. When you read a breaking putt, visualize the ball curving along the path and dropping into the cup. Picture the roll in your mind's eye from start to finish. Since your nonlinear personality makes it difficult for you to read the break to a certain spot like a linear putter can (your mind will tell you that the spot is the end point of your putt rather than the start), it's important that you shift your focus to the hole. This is your target.

## SOME EXTRA HELP

In order to be a successful nonlinear putter you must accurately determine the ball's entry point into the cup. The best way to do this is to convert the cup into a clock [photo, below]. Mark 6 o'clock as the point closest to the ball and 12 o'clock as the far side (with 9' o'clock on the left and 3 o'clock on the right). As you read the putt in full, don't try to figure out how much the putt will break, a move that turns the putt into a straight line (which goes against your personality). Instead, calculate at which time the ball will drop over the lip—at 5:15, 3:30, 8:45—and stay fixated on that entry point. The right side of your brain will fill in the dots.

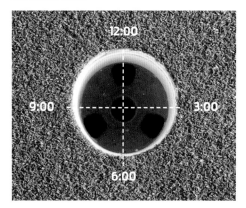

Picture the hole as a clock to help determine your entry point.

NONLINEAR TARGET

**NONLINEAR MUST**
Visualize the roll and focus on the entry point. That is your target.

# LINEAR PUTTING: HOW TO DO IT

### PRE-PUTT ROUTINE

Stand behind the ball, visualize your straight line to the high point of the break and then pick your spot either left (for left-to-right breaking putts) or right (for right-to-left breaking putts) of the hole. Since your linear personality allows you to aim at a single spot, be very specific in your read. Once you have your spot, don't lose focus of it. Aim the line on your ball to the spot and, while still keeping your eyes trained on your target, step into your address position. The steps are very important—aim first and then take your address.

If you need to make a few practice strokes, make them while looking down at your aim spot. But before you pull the trigger, use your sense of sight to track between your spot, an intermediate target and your putterface to make sure you're aimed correctly.

> "Since your linear personality allows you to aim at a single spot, be very specific in your read."

**EYES**
Never take them off your "spot."

**PUTTERFACE**
Aim it at your spot first, then take your address position.

**BALL**
Align the logo (or a line you've marked in pen) to your ball-spot line.

**INTERMEDIARY**
Choose an intermediate target a few inches in front of the ball that's also on your ball-spot line as an extra aiming measure.

## LINEAR PUTTING STEP-BY-STEP

**STEP 1**
Read the putt, choose your spot, and align the line on your ball or the logo along it.

**STEP 2**
Without losing focus on your spot, aim the putterface. Look between the putterface and your spot (as well as an intermediate target) a few times to make sure you're aimed correctly.

**STEP 3**
Once you're aimed, take your full address—remember, linear putters aim first and then build thier setup around the putterface. If you need to make a few practice strokes, do so with your eyes on your spot.

**STEP 4**
Give your spot and the putterface one more look to verify your aim (don't forget to make use of your intermediate target) and pull the trigger.

# NONLINEAR PUTTING: HOW TO DO IT

### PRE-PUTT ROUTINE

The routine for a nonlinear putter is much different than for a linear putter, with the most important change being that a nonlinear putter gets into his address position first and then starts the process of aiming—the exact opposite of a linear putter. Here's how to do it.

Stand behind the ball and track with your eyes your perceived roll of the ball from left to right or right to left into the cup. Then trace the same line coming back to your ball. Using this info, determine the entry point using the clock analogy explained on page 131. Fixate your eyes on the entry point and make a few practice strokes.

Next, address the ball and settle into your stance. Look back to the entry point and shuffle your stance until you feel that you're aimed appropriately. Since you're a nonlinear putter and you've pictured the roll and the entry point, your right brain will help you feel the break and settle you into the correct stance. Once you're set, look back at the ball and putt.

"A nonlinear putter gets into his address first and then aims—the opposite of a linear putter."

**EYES**
Keep them focused on the entry point.

**STANCE**
Get into your address first, then aim your putter so that it matches the roll you envisioned.

**ENTRY POINT**
Determine it by using the image of a clock. Once you have it, don't try to read break into your putt.

## NONLINEAR PUTTING STEP-BY-STEP

**STEP 1**
Visualize the ball's roll in your mind's eye. Trace the path back and through and determine the entry point.

**STEP 2**
With your eyes focused on the entry point, step into your address—don't worry about aiming your putter just yet.

**STEP 3**
Settle into your address position, still keeping your eyes fixated on the entry point. If you need to make a practice stroke, do so while looking at your target.

**STEP 4**
Now, aim your putter. Make sure to tap your sense of feel to guide your body and putterface into the proper positions. Drop your eyes back to the ball and make your stroke.

# AVOIDING CONFLICTS

**S I MENTIONED** earlier in this chapter, problems arise when you try to perform outside what your personality allows. Trouble also rears its head when you allow your non-personality traits to creep into your pre-putt and alignment routines. These are what I call linear and nonlinear conflicts, and they should be avoided at all costs.

## LINEAR CONFLICTS

Because linear putters have the ability to aim at their spot, it's important that they read break correctly (for help on this, consult Mark Sweeney's advice in Chapter 6). Perception is a very big part of putting. Some linear players see the putting surface as flatter than it really is, and some see it as more tilted than it really is. If you're a linear putter and you're rolling the ball where you intend, but it just isn't dropping into the cup on a consistent enough basis for you, it's highly probable that your reads are off. Here's how to correct the problem.

Find a curving putt on the practice putting green, give it your best read and select your spot. Drop a coin on your spot and then run a piece of string tied to two posts (tall tees or pencils will do the trick) over the ball and your spot *[photo, right]*. Go through your pre-putt routine, address the ball and putt down the string. If your read and ball speed were correct then the putt should fall into the cup. If your speed was correct and the putt missed, move the post at the spot to the left or right to add more break or take some away. Do this until the ball consistently drops into the cup when you make your stroke under the string line. Then compare the position of the post to the coin over your original spot. Determine the difference in percentages—this is your green-read handicap. (Don't compare the two in inches since the difference will change according to the length of the putt.) Use your green-read handicap on every putt. For example, if you discover that you over-read your putts by 10 percent using this test, then subtract 10 percent from each read you make on the course. You'll learn to adjust over time, so perform the test frequently so you know exactly where you're at with your green-reading accuracy.

## NONLINEAR CONFLICTS

Correcting aim problems for a nonlinear putter isn't so clear-cut. That's because nonlinear putters putt with their touch and feel senses, which are in constant battle with their sense of sight. Your feel senses tell you one thing, but your eyes tell you another, and the more attention you give your eyes, the more they'll interfere with your read. Nonlinear putters must learn to trust their feel and touch senses more than their eyes. It's difficult, especially for the inexperienced. The best thing to do is to hit the practice green, go through your pre-shot routine, and consciously tell yourself to shut off your left brain and go with what you feel. If you're ever over a putt that you think you've read correctly but at the last minute you look up and your eyes tell you something different, back off. For a nonlinear putter to putt his best, the feel and touch senses have to be trusted.

## WHY HAVEN'T I SEEN THIS BEFORE?

If you're wondering why it's taken so long to crack the left-right brain code in putting, it's because the linear putting method is very sound. So sound that it was the only thing taught for 70 years. It's logical—read the break to a certain spot and aim at that spot. Yet there was no denying the level of frustration experienced by amateurs and pros alike. I became very interested in the topic while working on a research project in the mid-1990s with a team of optometrists who were studying the effects of vision and dominant eye on putter aim. After a while we could make any player a perfect aimer on a straight 10-foot putt within a matter or minutes by moving the ball back or forward in the player's stance, and they could repeat their perfect aim over and over. On breaking putts, however, these perfect aimers couldn't aim at the side of a barn. The dilemma jump-started a second research project with dozens of sports psychologists who found that most players, even the ones with perfect aim on straight 10-footers, visualize in curved lines. This explained why our perfect straight-putt aimers in the first project erred so badly when they tried to aim at the same spot on a curve. They missed just like you did if you tested out as a nonlinear putter on page 129. We discovered a whole new breed of putting animal, one that standard teaching techniques had ignored. Until now.

**CONFLICT AVOIDANCE**
Gauge your green reading often to see if you're over-reading or under-reading break. For linear putters, green reading must be accurate for the system to work.

# 8

# Golf's Best Secret: The Long Putter

Long putters are often seen as controversial or in a negative light—a public acknowledgement that you've lost control of your nerves and your ability to putt the "right" way. The fact is, however, that their use has revitalized the games of many Tour and everyday players. Here's how to "go long."

# The Change Agent
# Scott Munroe

*GOLF Magazine Top 100 Teacher, Adios G.C., Coconut Creek, Fla./Nantucket G.C., Nantucket, Ma.*

Scott Munroe has seen both his professional and everyday students improve their putting statistics by using a long putter. Here he tells you the dos and don'ts of using the long boy, and explains away the reasons why you've held back from using one for so long.

**T**HE LONG PUTTER has been around since the late 1980s, when Charlie Owens started using one on the Senior Tour because he had a bad back. Since then, the professional tours have seen players reinvent and renew their putting games and win numerous Tour titles around the world. Vijay Singh, Fred Couples and Bernhard Langer, three of the finest players of their or any era, are convincing case studies for how a long putter can take your game back to (or beyond) a level you'd lost for good.

How do you know if you're a candidate for using a long putter? The truth is that everyone's a candidate. Here are just a few of the reasons:

● As we get older, back pain and stiffness becomes an issue in our games. If this is you, then you should try a long putter.
● A long putter is a fantastic teaching aid. In the late 1990s, Charlie Rymer, one of the best putters on the PGA Tour, competed with a standard-length putter, but practiced with a long putter.
● On fast modern greens, a long putter gives you greater consistency on the speed of your putts.
● I'll try to say this quietly so no one else hears us: You have the yips.

This chapter is not about how to tell if you have the yips or how to cure the yips (for that, see Chapter 10). Rather, think of this chapter as an owner's guide to improving your putting game with a long putter or a belly putter once you've made the decision to use one. That could well be the smartest decision you'll ever make in your life as a golfer.

## 5 Things I'll Teach You In This Chapter

**1** How to get fitted for a long putter.

**2** The Piston Stroke—the ultimate long-putter motion for smooth, easy putts.

**3** The Body Stroke, a technique that marries a more traditional motion with longer-length putters.

**4** Secrets for dominating on the green with your new weapon.

**5** The best long- and belly-putter practice drills.

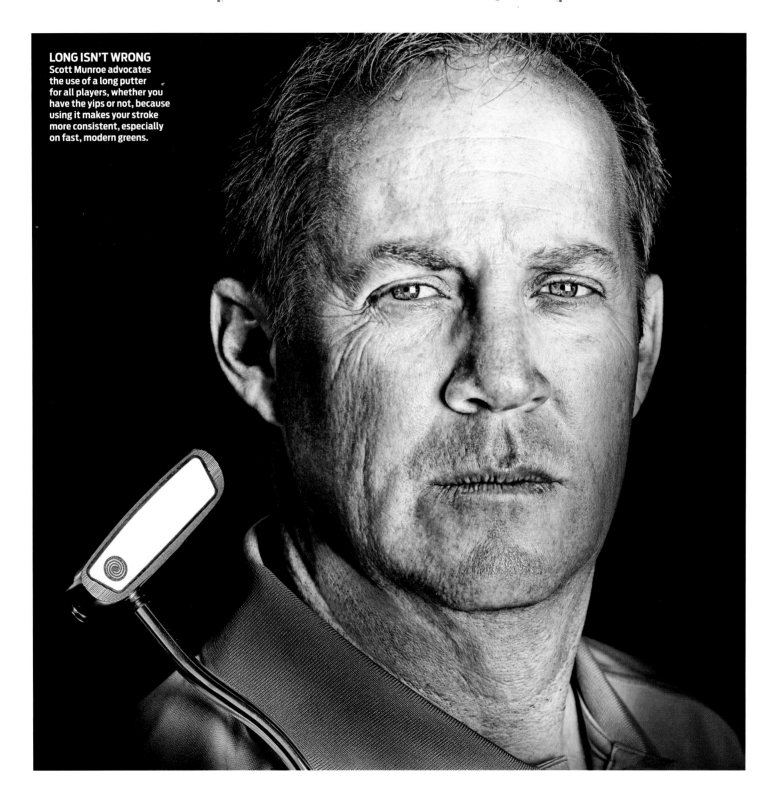

**LONG ISN'T WRONG**
Scott Munroe advocates
the use of a long putter
for all players, whether you
have the yips or not, because
using it makes your stroke
more consistent, especially
on fast, modern greens.

## ALL ABOUT ME

**Name:** Scott "Money" Munroe

**Teaching since:** 1977

**Where you can find me:** Adios G.C., Coconut Creek, Fla. (winter); Nantucket G.C., Nantucket Ma. (summer)

**Where I've played:** Georgia Southern University (1981-1985); Australian PGA Tour (1987-1990)

**Where I've taught:** Nicklaus-Flick Golf Schools (Australia and the U.S.); PGA National Golf Academy (Palm Beach Gardens, Fla.); ESPN Golf Schools

**Who I've instructed:** Notable students have included PGA Tour players Michael Allen, Jodie Mudd, Bernhard Langer, Guy Boros; and professional athletes Michael Jordan, Dan Marino, Ivan Lendl and Peyton Manning, among others

**Awards I've won:** *Golf Magazine's* Top 100 Teachers (2009-current); ESPN Top 25 Instructor

**My best contribution to the game:** Building a teaching method that translates to all handicaps, from new golfers to Tour professionals and that help students play well quickly

**For more instruction:** golf.com/ bestputtingbook moneygolf.net

# "Any time I place a long or belly putter in a student's hands, their stroke immediately becomes rhythmic and smooth."

**T**HERE ARE MANY things that can go wrong during your putting stroke. You can trace the wrong path, or unduly open or close the putterface. As many of the instructors in this book have already pointed out, you can err by making too long or too short of a backstroke and then decelerating or over-accelerating on the way through, destroying your ability to control distance. In my opinion, committing any of these mistakes is a result of not being able to appropriately feel the weight of the putterhead during your stroke. It's the same thing that happens with your full swing: If you can't feel the club, then you have no idea where it is and, more important, what you're going to do with it.

This reason alone is why you should consider investing in a long or belly putter. The special shape and design of these flatsticks makes it easy to feel the weight of the putterhead from start to finish. A standard extra-length putterhead weighs approximately 100 more grams than the same head fashioned for a regular-length shaft, and the longer shaft promotes a fluid back-and-through motion, like the sway of the pendulum on a grandfather clock. Any time I place a long or belly putter in a student's hands, their stroke immediately becomes more rhythmic and smooth.

The benefits of long putters can no longer be ignored. More and more professionals are putting them into play (including Tim Clark, who won the 2010 Players Championship at TPC Sawgrass using a long putter), and whereas once only a handful of specialty manufacturers offered them, now almost every major club brand has a long boy. The trend is picking up so much steam that it can no longer be considered a trend—long putters are legitimate tools to get the ball in the hole on a consistent basis across all skill levels.

When choosing a long putter it's important that you find one that looks good to you, because that breeds confidence. The next priority is to find one with a sole that sits flat on the ground with the shaft hitting your sternum once you assume your address position. If you have a bad back, it can be longer, but the sternum is ideal. If you can't find one that's the proper length or lie for you, don't settle! Any trained fitter can make the necessary changes to a long putter. All of this, except the sternum part—also holds true for a belly putter.

One thing you'll notice immediately is that most long putters are face balanced, so you'll have much less of an arc in the path of your stroke than if you're accustomed to playing with a toe-weighted putter. Also, long putters are built with significanly greater lie angle, which encourages more of a straight-back-and-through stroke.

Once you purchase a long or belly putter, fool around with various stroke styles and methods that feel good to you on the practice green. My whole philosophy on putting is to do whatever works. In this chapter we'll go over two popular ways to swing your long or belly putter, the Body Stroke and the Piston Stroke *[photos, right]*, but I want to emphasize that it's okay to experiment and find what works for you. My good friend Mark Officer was a fellow player on the Aussie Tour back in the Dark Ages (you know, before metal woods and long putters), and he's the inventor of the Perfect Stroke teaching aid and one of the great putting teachers going today. We agree on many things, and one of them is the "do whatever works" philosophy. The fundamentals have to be there, but after that you can develop your own style.

## WATCH & LEARN

When you see this icon, go to **golf.com/bestputting book** fro a free video lesson from long-putter teacher Scott Munroe.

**THE BODY STROKE:** An adaption of a traditional putting motion that emphasizes powering the club with your core muscles and by rocking your shoulders. This stroke can be used with both belly *[pictured]* and long putters.

**THE PISTON STROKE:** By anchoring the butt of a long putter or belly putter in your sternum and using your right arm to power the club, you create a one-lever pendulum that makes it nearly impossible to swing the putter off line.

# ADDRESSING THE BALL WITH YOUR LONG PUTTER

**AS YOU CAN** guess, setting up to use your long putter involves a few twists on your standard address in order to compensate for the longer shaft length. If you're using a long putter, the primary key is to anchor the butt of the club in your sternum *[photos, right]*. If you're using a belly putter, the trick is to match your setup to the type of stroke that you're going to put into play. For the Piston Stroke, anchor the butt of your belly putter in your sternum; for the Body Stroke, anchor the butt of your belly putter in your belly *[photos, opposite page]*. These setup positions are easy to get down with just a little bit of practice, especially if you adhere to the following rules:

● Position the ball in your stance so it's just slightly left of the center of your torso if you're using a long putter, and in the center of your stance if you're using a belly putter. Make a mental check every time you position the ball because it's critical to getting the smooth strike you want.

● Bend over from your shoulders and let them slouch. This is important because it helps you relax, and since you're not all hunched over like you would be with a standard length putter, you might feel a little stiff. Slouching your

**LONG PUTTER ADDRESS**
Bend forward so the butt of the club hits your sternum when the club is soled on the ground.

shoulders will take the tension out of your setup.

● Keep your right elbow close to your side. You don't want that thing sticking out like you're doing some sort of chicken dance. Feel that elbow in there all nice and snug.

● You don't want to feel any tension in your body, but you do want to feel like your abs, your butt and your legs are firm and solid, because you don't want to have any lower-body movement whatsoever when you make your stroke.

> "Bend over from your shoulders and let them slouch. This helps you relax."

**BALL FORWARD**
Since the long putter is designed to be swung like a pendulum, position the ball forward so you catch it on a slight upswing after your stroke bottoms out.

SWING BOTTOM

# THE LEFT-HAND O.K. GRIP

**BELLY OPTIONS**
Set the butt of the club in your sternum for a Piston Stroke *[above]* and in your belly for a Body Stroke *[right]*, with the ball centered in your stance.

Anchor the club on the left side of your torso in either setup to create a forward shaft lean at address.

**AN IMPORTANT** part of setting up with a long putter for either stroke or with a belly putter for the Piston Stroke is the positioning of your left hand.

While there are a variety of right hand grips you can use with long and belly putters (and some of them are pretty funky, as you'll see on the next page), there's really only one left hand grip you can use that's fundamentally sound enough to produce the motion you need.

First set the putterhead flat on the ground and balance the shaft with your right hand. Next, make the universal "O.K." symbol with your left hand and place it over the very end of the butt of the club. Adjust your thumb so that it rests on top of your index finger and points away from your target. Now simply wrap the rest of your fingers around the shaft and place your left hand against your sternum. You're ready to apply any of the right-hand grips on the following pages.

**NOTE:** If you decide to use a belly putter in combination with the Body Stroke, then you don't have to worry about this part of your setup.

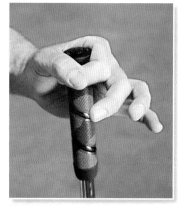

**STEP 1:** Set your left hand on top of the grip using an "O.K." symbol.

**STEP 2:** Wrap the rest of your left-hand fingers around the handle.

**STEP 3:** Set the club in your belly or sternum and add your right hand.

# RIGHT-HAND GRIP: VARIETY IS EVERYTHING

**THE PLAYERS WHO** innovated golf by starting to use the long putter brought other innovations into the game along with it. The sheer variety of methods for gripping the club with your right hand even spawned the "claw" grip that some Tour players use on standard-length putters. Remembering that you should go with whatever works in putting, experiment with the following grips and see which one feels best and, more importantly, produces the best results. Each has a unique feel and effect on your motion, so there's no way to tell if one is better than the others until you try them all.

For starters, get into your address without a putter and let your arms dangle. Check the way your right arm hangs; with some people the right hand rotates inward and with others it turns outward. That's your first clue for deciding which right-hand hold to use. Also, the grip that best keeps your right elbow next to your side should rise to the top of your list.

## LONG-PUTTER AND PISTON-STROKE GRIPS

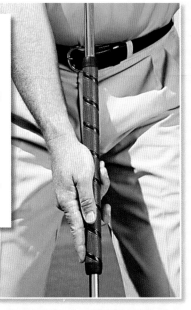

**TRADITIONAL**
The "fatty" part of your palm (near your thumb) is on top of the grip, your thumb is on top of the grip, and your index finger is extended flat against the grip. This is the most natural way to position your right hand because it resembles the way you grip all of your other clubs.

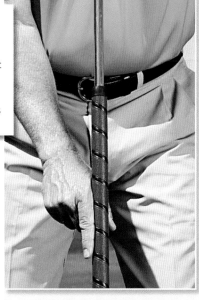

**PENCIL GRIP**
Your thumb is actually behind the shaft with this one, with the shaft resting between it and your index finger. The side of your index finger is against the shaft.

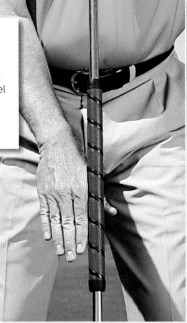

**SAW GRIP**
Your thumb is behind the shaft again, but all four of your other fingers are parallel to the shaft, with the side of your index finger touching it.

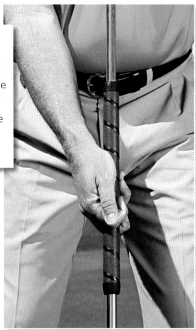

**FORK GRIP**
Here your thumb is back on top and the shaft is in your palm, but you place the shaft between your index and middle fingers (like you're stabbing food with the tines on a fork.

## BELLY-PUTTER GRIP OPTIONS FOR BODY STROKE

**THE GRIPS AT LEFT** can be used with a long putter with either stroke, and with a belly putter/Piston Stroke combination. If you feel more comfortable using a belly putter with a Body Stroke, a combination that best mimics the standard putting motion, then experiment with the holds below.

### PUSH GRIP
Exactly like the pencil grip, but your index finger is flat against the shaft.

### MAMA-MIA GRIP
You wrap your thumb and index finger around the shaft with their tips touching, bend your middle finger so that the middle of it is flush against the shaft, and place the tips of your last two fingers on top of the shaft.

### TRADITIONAL GRIP
A standard putting grip with the butt of the club anchored by your stomach.

### LEFT-HAND-LOW GRIP
Puts your left hand in the "lead" or dominant position, which is useful since you want your left hand to dominate a traditional putting stroke.

### SPLIT GRIP
Helps eliminate wristiness by forcing you to generate all the power in the stroke by rocking your shoulders.

### DADDY LONGLEGS GRIP
Anchors the shaft against the inside of your left arm—the ultimate grip for removing wristiness from your stroke.

**BACKSTROKE**

**ONE LEVER**
Swing the putter back with your right arm only— keep the rest of your body very still.

**STRAIGHT BACK**
Since your goal is to create a perfect pendulum, swing the putterhead straight back along the target line.

# HOW TO MAKE A PISTON STROKE

**WITH THE PISTON** stroke, your goal is to limit your moving body parts to a single one: your right arm. Notice at address how your right shoulder is slightly lower than your left due to the fact that you reach farther down the shaft with your right arm, and how your left elbow is pointed at your target while your left forearm is parallel to the ground. The trick to making a successful Piston Stroke is to maintain all of these positions for the duration of your stroke while motoring the club with only your right arm.

Grip the club very lightly with your right hand using the grip of your choice, and—this is key—keep your right elbow tight to your side with some slight flex in it. Your entire body should remain completely still during this stroke with the exception of your right arm.

**FORWARD-STROKE**

**PUSH FORWARD**
Use your right arm as a piston and push the putterhead straight at the target.

**STEADY BODY**
You'll create the smoothest pendulum possible when you limit your body action to your right arm from start to finish.

The body has to be completely still. When you go to make your stroke, think of your right arm as a piston. Take the putter back with a slight bending of your right arm, then simply push your right arm out to the target until it's fully extended. When you finish your stroke, your left arm and right arm should form a 45-degree angle. Using your right arm as a piston like this while anchoring the butt of the club against your sternum (or your belly if you're using a belly putter) creates a perfect pendulum motion back and through. You can't miss.

**"Limit your moving body parts to your right arm."**

**BACKSTROKE**

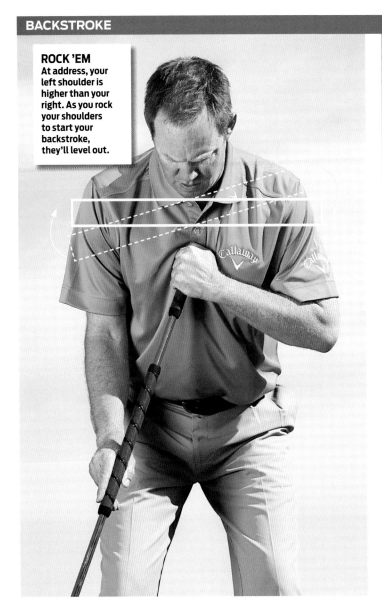

**ROCK 'EM**
At address, your left shoulder is higher than your right. As you rock your shoulders to start your backstroke, they'll level out.

**BODY ACTION**
Although your shoulders are the main power producers, tie in your core muscles and your lats to smoothen out your stroke.

# HOW TO MAKE A BODY STROKE

**THERE'S NO QUESTION** this stroke is more difficult to execute, but it may feel better to you, particularly with a belly putter (although there's no reason why you shouldn't experiment with this motion using a long putter as well).

This stroke is essentially a rocking motion of your shoulders, but you don't want to consciously say to yourself, "move your shoulders now." Rather, you want to feel this movement from the inside out—from your stomach muscles and lateral muscles. You want those

muscles to feel taut—not ridiculously tense, but taut and quiet. In your back stroke, your left shoulder will rock down (and your right up) until both of your shoulders are level. In your forward-stroke, your right shoulder rocks down (and the left up) until your left shoulder

**FORWARD-STROKE**

**REVERSE ROCK**
On the way back to the ball, reverse the rocking action. Finish with your left shoulder higher then your right.

**MUSCLE PULL**
If you do It correctly, your stomach muscles will feel taut, especially i n your through-stroke and as you hold your finish.

is once again higher than your right.

The secret to making this rocking action without moving your putter off line is to move as a single unit. There are no independent parts in this stroke. Everything moves in unison—your shoulders, core and lats. Since your putterhead rises off the ground going back and through with this stroke, pay careful attention to your ball position. Playing it too far forward will cause you to strike the ball too much on an upswing; playing it too far back will force you to hit too much down on the ball.

One reason why you get such a smooth roll with a long putter is that you set the grip against your belly or sternum. This creates a fulcrum, and a fulcrum tends to add rotation. You might not feel it, but it happens, and actually is a requirement for solid putting

"This is key—keep your right elbow tight to your right side with some slight flex in it."

**PRIORITY NO. 1**
Regardless of the type of putter you put into play or the stroke motion you use to roll the ball, you must keep your right elbow in tight.

# THE RULES OF BEING A MONEY PUTTER

**WE'VE GONE OVER** a lot of material in a short amount of time, but if you spend time working on your setup and your left-hand hold while experimenting with your right-hand grip and variations on either stroke, you'll get good with your belly or long putter in no time. These things really are easy to use and personalize. As you continue to practice, keep the following 10 rules in mind. They're the last remaining pieces to dominating with your long putter.

**1.** Keep your right elbow glued to your right side. It will slide across the front of your body as you extend your stroke after impact, but you won't even have to think about it. This is rule number one for a reason: By keeping your right elbow tucked, you give your stroke a guide and keep the clubhead on path.

**2.** Never think about making the putt. Think about making a good stroke.

**3.** Speed is more important than line, and line is simple if you're a good aimer.

**4.** Long putters typically produce a purer roll. As such, it's very likely that you'll have to play less break since the ball will be moving faster compared to the roll you get with a standard putter.

**5.** Great putters usually don't have short backswings and long follow-throughs. Keep it even.

**6.** Feel like you are "dropping" the putter on the ball.

**7.** Keep your head down. Stroke the putter past your left toe and listen for the ball to go in.

**8.** Use firmer grip pressure on slow greens and long putts. Use lighter grip pressure on fast greens and short putts.

**9.** When you're practicing your stroke, don't putt to a hole. That's just practicing missing putts. Work on your stroke to a spot on the green or a coin.

**10.** Constantly experiment—you never know what you may come up with.

**TRIAL & ERROR**
There are so many good options when using a long putter—length, grip and stroke—that practice actually becomes fun as you tinker with each part of your setup and motion.

# 9

# How to Practice for Improvement

The best place to improve your putting is on the practice green, but most players don't know how to work effectively. The only way you'll see lasting results is to pattern your practice based on the challenges you'll face on the course. Once you do that, getting your mind, eyes and body ready is easy.

# The Putt Doctor
# Craig Farnsworth

*PGA Tour putting coach, See and Score Golf Schools, The Palms G.C., La Quinta, Calif.*

Even great putters go awry, and skills come and go with the passing of time, making practice every bit as important as actually playing. Golf's leading sports vision expert is on the case with a practice regimen to keep your putting game razor sharp in seven key areas.

**P**UTTING PRACTICE, for the most part, is an afterthought for the majority of recreational players. I rarely see any reason in their technique. This is bad news because aimlessly stroking balls to the same hole without working on anything doesn't produce meaningful results. When I see a player doing this I always look at them and think, "Wouldn't it be prudent to shore up your alignment? How about using a mirror to make sure your setup is accurate? Why don't you have some kind of plan?"

I can go on with a number of reasons why the customary practice habits of most recreational players do little to help them improve, but the important thing to understand is that if you want to get better, you need to practice with a mind toward improving specific areas of your putting game. By understanding your tendencies and weaknesses, you can counter them with practice sessions geared toward a higher level of consistency and efficiency.

When I work with my students I recommend that each incorporate certain "rules" into every practice session. The first is to have a plan for practice, which should include your goals for improvement, the specific focus of the practice sessions and a record of your results. In addition, I feel 5 to 15 minutes per drill is enough. Another rule is to never respond to error. Accept that you're going to fail at times and learn from it. Don't allow your emotions to override this learning. Finally, no practice is complete without working on your routine or mental focus.

## 5 Things I'll Teach You In This Chapter

**1** How to repeatedly set up and align correctly at address.

**2** How to make sure your grip—your lone connection to the club—is correct.

**3** How to get in the correct mind-set to make putts on a more consistent basis.

**4** How to shore up your mechanics and speed control.

**5** How to improve your visualization skills— the Tour-player way to hole more putts.

**THE DOCTOR IS IN**
Dr. Craig Farnsworth has been
a trusted putting guru to more
than 125 Tour professionals,
including Nick Faldo, Annika
Sorenstam and Brad Faxon.
Utilize his focused drills to
improve every aspect of your
performance on the greens.

## ALL ABOUT ME

***Name:*** Dr. Craig L. Farnsworth

***Teaching since:*** 1998

***Where you can find me:*** See and Score Golf Schools, The Palms G.C., La Quinta, Calif.

***Where I've taught:*** Jim McLean, Nicklaus-Flick and Ritson-Sole golf schools; have instructed trainers for the U.S. Olympic Training Center, the U.S. Secret Service, Armed Forces, and U.S. Air Marshals

***Who I've instructed:*** Nick Faldo, Annika Sorenstam, Brad Faxon, Y.E. Yang, Paul Azinger, Brian Gay, Chip Beck and others

***Awards I've Won:*** Sullivan H.S. (Ind.) Athletic Hall of Fame (2005); Sports Vision Optometrist of the Year (1991)

***My best contribution to the game:*** More than 90% of all PGA Tour pros use my techniques; created a computer diagnostic system to analyze putting performance; wrote two best-selling books, *See It & Sink It* and *The Putting Prescription*

***For more instruction:*** golf.com/bestputtingbook
puttdoctor.com

**With student and longtime friend Nick Faldo.**

> **"Try these drills not only because they'll help your putting, but because they'll help you learn about your tendencies."**

**THERE ARE SEVEN** specific areas of your putting game that you need to practice in order to improve your results: setup, grip, alignment, stroke mechanics, speed, mental skills and greenreading. In this chapter I'll give you specific drills designed to address each one (except greenreading—all of the information you need here is in Chapter 6). I strongly recommend you experiment with these drills and techniques if you want to get better, particularly if one or more relate to one of your weaknesses. In general, however, I think it's well worth your while to try each of the drills, not only because they'll help your putting, but because they'll help you learn about your tendencies. Once you're aware of your typical mistakes, you'll have a much better chance of correcting them.

The first thing you need to address is your setup. If your stance and posture aren't solid, you have little chance of ever becoming a decent putter. Many of the amateur players I work with make one major mistake: they allow their arms to separate from one another at address and get too far away from their body. This fundamental error can make your stroke too handsy and inefficient. I'll show you a simple and easy way to remedy this problem right off the bat.

Next you'll have to work on your grip, which right now is likely too tight. Strangling the putter is an extremely common mistake and it can cause a number of problems, not the least of which is a loop that occurs between the backstroke and forward-stroke. This is a serious no-no, but once you try my grip-pressure test you'll feel more relaxed and natural throughout your stroke.

Once you have a solid address and grip you'll need to work on your alignment. Obviously, this is part of your setup, but I like to deal with it separately because it requires separate drills. If you're not a very good putter right now I can almost guarantee that your alignment is faulty and that you have some built-in compensations that don't work consistently. Once you master my alignment drills that will be a thing of the past.

At this point your setup, alignment and grip will be well on their way to recovery, and I'll introduce you to my drills for improving both your mental and mechanical approaches to putting. A common misconception about putting is that a proper mind-set alone, or just a sound stroke, is all anyone needs to succeed. You need to have both things correct if you want to hole a lot of putts.

Finally we'll cover arguably the most important aspect of putting: speed control. This is the real secret of most great putters—at least 70 percent of your practice time should be spent performing the speed drills in this chapter. Along with these exercises you'll find an explanation of my In-Vision-ing technique, used extensively on all professional tours. In-Vision-ing involves more than just seeing the line or the ball's roll. It's a whole-body experience that involves the way a particular putt behaves in relation to your typical stroke. If you have a hard time seeing putts drop in your mind's eye, this can be invaluable.

### WATCH & LEARN

When you see this icon go to to **golf.com/bestputtingbook** for a video lesson with vision expert Dr. Craig Farnsworth.

### THE 3 RULES OF PUTTING PRACTICE

**1.** Have a plan—set goals, record results, track progress.

**2.** Keep it compact—never practice a drill for more than 15 minutes or you'll risk losing focus.

**3.** Accept mistakes—that's why you're practicing, right?

**SEE IT, PRACTICE IT, SINK IT**
Getting the right perspective can
have a lot to do with success and
failure. Learn to use your eyes and
your practice time properly and you
should feel much more confident
and secure about your putting.

# 1. HOW TO PRACTICE YOUR SETUP

**TO MAKE AN** effective putting stroke you must have a solid, effective setup, which includes your stance and posture. There are several keys to ensuring a solid setup, but to begin you must have your arms "connected." By this I mean they need to be as close together as possible, but not so close that they create tension in your arms and shoulders (keep your shoulders, arms and elbows soft at all times). They also need to be inside the lines of your torso. If your arms are too much at your sides they can get "stuck" during the stroke.

## DO THIS:
## CONNECTION DRILL
To make sure your arms are properly in front of you at address, extend them straight out from your shoulder sockets so the shaft of your putter is parallel to the ground *[photo, below]*. You should do this first every time you address the ball before stroking a putt.

Stand straight up with your elbows in close and your arms stretched in front of you...

## THEN DO THIS:
## SQUARE DRILL
The second step to a solid setup is to make sure that your head, eyes, and shoulders are square to the target line. By doing so you'll allow the big muscles in your body to work effectively without the little ones getting in the way. I like to say, "Look up to square up." This should be a regular part of your address routine. As you address the ball with your arms and putter extended, you need to make sure your eyes, head and shoulders are square to the target line. If you're looking straight ahead in the direction your arms and putter are facing, you'll be in a good position.

Next, bend at the hips with your butt sticking out a bit *[photo, right]* and get your eyes over or inside the ball. A good way to ingrain

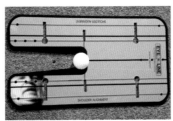

the correct position is to place an alignment mirror on the ground (the underside of an old CD also does the trick). The actual position of your eyes is best determined by which head and eye position allows you to perceive the line of the putt accurately. Most importantly, get your face parallel to the ground by tucking your chin, but don't lower your back or neck. This "face-parallel-to-the-earth" position will allow you to perceive the target line much more clearly.

...then bend from your hips and stick out your rear end a bit. This will help ensure that your eyes and shoulders are parallel to your target line.

### KEYS TO A SOLID SETUP
1. Extend your arms and putter so they're in front of your body and within your body lines.
2. Square your head and eyes to the target line—everything should be set parallel to your target line.
3. Bend from the hips so your eyes are over or just inside the ball.

# 2. HOW TO PRACTICE TAKING YOUR GRIP

**WHEN YOUR GRIP** pressure is too tight (more than five on a scale from one to ten), you'll tend to take the putter back too far and too fast. You'll likely also make a loop in your motion as you move from your backstroke to your forward-stroke. Getting this right, as well as placing your hands on the handle in such a way that your grip allows you to make a free and natural stroke, is the fast track to improved putting performance.

## DO THIS: GRIP CHECK

Take your putter in the palm of your bottom hand only (the right for right-handed players), making sure the putter handle runs through your wrist and not outside your forearm. This should form a straight line between your hand, wrist and forearm. Achieving this neutral position is critical, and you should check it often. Practice taking your grip while standing to the right of a full-length mirror. You'll know your grip is correct when you look back into the mirror over your right shoulder and see the straight line of the puttershaft running through the bottom of your wrist.

## THEN DO THIS: PRESSURE CHECK

Now place your top hand on the grip, making sure the handle is also in your palm. I suggest a reverse-overlapping grip, with the index finger of your top hand resting lightly over the pinkie of your bottom hand or between the pinkie and the ring finger.

Once you have both hands on the handle, check your grip pressure by making continuous practice strokes with your eyes closed.

Start off by gripping the handle with maximum pressure, then slowly reduce the pressure, never stopping your strokes, until you can start to feel the weight of the putterhead as it swings back and through (usually a 4 or 5 on a 1-to-10 scale).

If your grip pressure is too light, you'll find yourself re-gripping the club, usually at the start of the forward-stroke. With an overly tight grip all you feel is the handle, not the putterhead.

**CHECK #1**
Grip the handle in both palms, not your fingers.

**CHECK #2**
Putter handle runs through the bottom of the forearms, not outside the forearms.

**CHECK #3**
Straight line between your right hand, wrist and forearm.

# 3. HOW TO PRACTICE YOUR ALIGNMENT

**PROPER ALIGNMENT IS** as important, if not more so, than any other aspect of putting. If you're not aligned correctly, you have very little chance of putting consistently.

### DO THIS: CALIBRATE YOUR EYES

To become confident in your alignment, begin by finding a straight three- or four-foot putt that's relatively flat. Establish a straight line to the hole with a chalk line or two clubs placed parallel to the target line *[photo, right]*. Go through your setup checklist and then look directly down the target line so you get a real sense of a straight line to the hole. In your mind, trace the line that the putt will take to the hole at the pace you expect it to travel. Note what it looks like to be aligned correctly to the target, with your body parallel to the target line. This is what you want to re-create when you're out on the course.

Next, stroke a few putts to appreciate what it's like to putt when you're aimed accurately to the target, then remove the clubs or chalk line. If you choose to align the logo of your ball as an aiming device, make sure it's aimed correctly before you remove the guidance device you've chosen to use. Once you've done this your aim to the target should still appear accurate. If not, you can bet that your setup is off or you're using the wrong part of the putterhead to aim. To remedy the situation, remember to square up your eyes and shoulders by looking up with your head facing straight ahead, then look back down to the ball. Now, see which part of your putter appears to be aimed correctly. In particular, is it the line or lines on the putter, or is it the putterface? For most people it is only one or the other.

> **NOTE:** When working on your alignment, be aware that ball position can significantly affect your perspective. Moving the ball slightly back or forward in your stance can make it look like you're aimed right or left of the target.

**AIM GAME**
If you use a line on your ball to help with your alignment, draw a "T," point the stem along the target line and square your putterface to the top line. As you line it up you may find that closing your non-dominant eye makes the perspective more accurate than when you use both eyes.

# 4. HOW TO PRACTICE YOUR MENTAL SKILLS

**GETTING INTO THE** correct mind-set is a prerequisite for being an effective putter. Performance encompasses not only what you do physically but also what you're thinking during the stroke. Controlling your mind during this all-important second or so goes a long way toward controlling your body as well.

## DO THIS: NOWHERE DRILL

Stroke a putt with no target in sight *[photo, right]*. Just get used to stroking the putt without any concern for making or missing. Repeat four times. Note how little tension you feel while stroking these putts without a target.

Next, set up to an actual hole and imagine hitting the putt to win your club championship (role playing like this is a great way to work on controlling your thinking). Attempt to stroke the putt with the same tension level as the putt you hit to no target. After you stroke the putt, close your eyes and try to feel if you actually stroked the putt with the same amount of tension as the putt to nowhere. If you didn't, repeat the first part of the drill with no target. Continue until you can stroke one putt to nowhere and then one to the target with the same low level of tension.

When you go out to play, recall the tension level you had while putting to nowhere and try to make this your only focus during your stroke. Keep in mind that there are few things under your control in this great game. Your tension level is one that you can learn to control with practice. Bear in mind that the best tension killer is drawing a positive mind's-eye picture of the ball rolling into the cup.

**PUTT FREE**
The simple act of putting to no target teaches you the low-tension mind-set you need for success.

Use an intermediate target to remain focused on the task at hand without prematurely peeking—a sure sign of an anxious mind-set.

## THEN DO THIS: SPOT ALIGN

Another great drill to improve your mental outlook is designed to prevent you from peeking at the hole before or during impact. This mistake reflects an anxious mind-set and can be detrimental to your putting success. To overcome this "quick look" tendency, find a spot a couple of inches in front of the ball on your target line, or make one with a tee or a Sharpie *[photo, left]*. This spot is your mental and visual focus point during your stroke.

As you stand behind the ball looking down the target line, move directly into your setup while keeping the spot in focus. If you need to take a practice stroke do it before you walk into your setup, but don't lose your concentration on the pen mark or tee. Just before your actual stroke, shift your visual focus away from the ball to the spot. Now stroke the ball with your only goal being to attempt to roll the putt over your intermediate target (you should always *attempt* tasks—you can't always focus on goals).

Practicing this drill will focus your mind on getting the ball to roll over the spot instead of trying to make the putt. This change in focus removes much of the tension and anxiety players experience on the greens and greatly improves their results.

# 5. HOW TO PRACTICE YOUR STROKE

**YES, SOME PLAYERS** actually think of mechanics during the stroke, but for the most part, good putters think of nothing other than seeing the ball go in the hole. Work on your mechanics on the practice green so you can be free to trust your stroke on the course. To begin, I recommend trying my string and needles drill, which will teach you to consistently get the ball started on the proper line. Master this ability and your stroke—and mind—will be much freer.

### DO THIS: STRING DRILL

Start by attaching a length of string to two knitting needles (you can also use pencils or a simple chalk line). The string should be 12 to 15 feet in length. Find a nice flat spot on the practice green and plant the needles into the turf so the string is about six-inches above the ground. One of the needles should be just behind a hole and the other should be on the other side so that the string runs directly over the cup *[photo, right]*.

Place a ball directly under the string approximately ten feet or so from the hole. Now align your putter to the target line and stroke a few putts. If you have difficulty getting the ball on line consistently, then your mechanics need some help. Continue to practice this drill until you can get the ball rolling straight down the string and into the hole on a consistent basis.

Another value of this drill is that it will show you your tendencies. Most players don't push or pull their putts on an equal basis, so once you know what your mistake tends to be you can adjust. If you find that you tend to push

**CHECK**
Use the string to check if your dominant miss is a push or pull, then adjust accordingly.

**LINE 'EM UP**
Square the face to the string with the ball directly under the ine.

your putts, you're probably taking the club back too much with your hands, which opens the putterface to the path. Instead, concentrate on powering the clubhead with your arms and shoulders. Also, you might be playing the ball too far back in your stance. Try moving it forward to remedy the problem.

### THEN DO THIS: BIG MUSCLE DRILL

If you find you're pulling putts, you might be playing the ball too far forward in your stance. Move it back a bit, or weaken your top hand. Another cause for pulled putts is an overly handsy stroke. If you think this is your problem, try placing a ball between your right wrist and the butt of your putter's grip *[photo, above]*. Stroke a few putts with the ball trapped between your wrist and the grip. This encourages you to use your big muscles instead of the little ones, which are difficult to control.

> "Good putters think of nothing but seeing the ball go in the hole."

**SPEED DEMON**
As you sink putts from all four points, assess your speed. Most players do better at short and mid-range putts when they roll the ball with enough speed to hit the middle or the back of the cup.

**DON'T DECELERATE**
One reason golfers miss short putts is that they take the putter too far back and then decelerate coming forward. You're much better off using a shorter overall stroke length

# 6. HOW TO PRACTICE SPEED ON SHORT TO MID-RANGE PUTTS

**IF YOU WANT** to be a good putter, the majority of your practice sessions should be spent learning to control speed. This includes putts inside of ten feet, as well as from longer distances. Since four- and five-footers are the nemesis of most amateurs, I suggest you start there.

### DO THIS: QUAD DRILL
Begin by setting up four tees surrounding a practice hole from four equidistant points *[photo, above]*. Once you set up the tees, putt one ball from each of the four points and see how many you make. I suggest doing this drill three times in succession so you can get a real sense of what speed is best for making each putt.

After you complete the drill, think about which speed was most effective. Did you do best when the ball just trickled over the edge of the lip, or did you make more putts when the ball rolled into the hole with enough pace to hit the back or middle of the cup? I bet you'll find that dying the ball into the hole wasn't as effective. This is particularly true if there is a break to any of the putts. What you'll notice is that a more aggressive approach works better, but that your aim has to be different than when you try to die it in the hole.

So how do you gain enough confidence to make these short putts with an aggressive stroke? I suggest picturing the putt rolling into the hole at the right speed in your mind's eye when you're at address. Then when you actually stroke the putt, just keep that picture in your mind and try to re-create it. It works for PGA Tour pros, and it will work for you.

> **NOTE:** Once you feel comfortable holing all four putts from four feet, move the tees back to six feet. Lengthening the distance will only sharpen your speed control and confidence. Once you can consistently make putts from six feet, everything from four feet and in will seem easy.

# 7. HOW TO PRACTICE SPEED ON LONG PUTTS

**LEARNING TO CONTROL** your speed on long putts is one of the most important aspects of putting, particularly if you've found you have a propensity for three-putting. Long-distance control and accuracy are important because the majority of amateurs lack the ability to hit approach shots consistently close to the hole—at least close enough for an easy two-putt. Studies show that the average player three-putts five times per round. You need to start bucking this trend.

## DO THIS:
### THREE-TARGET DRILL

One of my favorite drills to develop better distance control and speed on long putts is my three-target test. To set it up, place three tees or divot repair tools on a practice green at least thirty feet from your start point. I suggest distances of 35, 45 and 55 feet *[photo, right]*.

Now, take three balls and putt one to each distance. Step off the distance from the intended target that each ball stopped and add up the numbers. Try the drill again, this time stopping to feel exactly how hard you hit each putt.

If you find that you struggle to reproduce the desired speed, it's very likely that your hands are too active in your stroke. This type of action makes it very difficult to control distance, especially on the longer ones. If you don't improve relatively quickly (i.e., your miss distance totals remain static) you might want to try a pencil-type grip *[photo, above]*, which effectively take the hands out of the stroke and makes your motion more rhythmic, especially during your transition.

**PENCIL GRIP**
This hold takes your hands out of the stroke, making it easy to control distance, especially on long putts.

## THEN DO THIS:
### DISTANCE CHECK

Another reason you might struggle with long putts is faulty perception. As an optometrist, I've found that most golfers see the location of the hole as closer than it really is. This results in a lot of putts that end up well short of the target.

To counteract this problem, stand off to the side of the line before you start putting *[photo, above]* and track the ball's roll to the hole in your mind's eye. You'll probably notice that the distance between the ball and the cup appears longer than what you calculated standing behind the hole. Keep in mind how far the putt looked from this angle and then go back and start the drill over. I'm willing to bet your results will be better after you've judged the distance from this new position.

> **"Most golfers see the location of the hole as closer than it really is."**

# BONUS: HOW TO PRACTICE VISUALIZING

**IN-VISION-ING IS** a technique I developed that allows your eyes and brain to inform your body how hard to hit a given putt. The technique involves tracking your eyes over the line of the putt at the same speed you want the putt to roll. But using just your eyes is only the beginning. Through study and experimentation I've found that using your eyes and your hands in tandem actually impacts the brain more than the eyes alone. Here's how.

## DO THIS: TRACKING DRILL
Stand to the side of the target line, half way between the ball and the cup. First, analyze the terrain and the distance with your eyes as I've described. Then grip your putter and point the putterhead at the ball. Now move the putter toward the cup at a speed you believe necessary to sink the putt *[photos, right]*. You should end with the toe of your putter pointing at the hole at the moment your imaginary putt drops into the hole. By moving your eyes from the ball to the hole at the proper speed, you'll enhance your brain's ability to move your arms and putter with the right amount of energy.

## THEN DO THIS: PAY ATTENTION
One of the best ways to practice your visualization skills is to watch other players putt to cups from longer distances on the putting green. Track the roll of the ball off their putterface until it stops. Better yet, imagine the roll of their putt before it's struck and then predict, as quickly as possible after impact, whether the putt is going to be long, short or perfect.

**TRACK MAN**
For the ultimate visualization experience, stand between the ball and the hole and point your putter at the ball...

**DON'T RUSH IT**
When I first ask students to try this drill they always err on the fast side. For example, they'll track a 50-foot putt in 2 seconds, when in reality it takes a ball 5 seconds to roll 50 feet on a flat surface with the right pace.

...then move your putter to the hole at the same speed as the perceived roll. Your real putt and your imaginary putt should reach the cup at the same time.

# 10

# How to Fix Your Worst Flaws

There are mistakes and then there are *faults*—major glitches in your putting system that make it difficult to get the ball near the cup. We're talking about the yips and other misfires like choking and freezing that can ruin careers, and for which there is no cure. That is, until now.

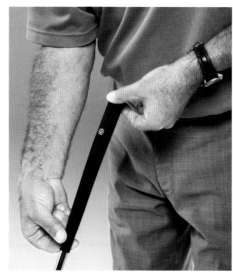

# The Research Brain
# Marius Filmalter

*Golf Magazine putting contributor, PGA Tour putting coach and researcher, Marius Golf, Dallas, Tex.*

My access to research data on 50,000 putting strokes puts me in a unique position: I know what good putters do and bad putters don't. I also know where the game's most damaging faults take root. With this information, curing big-time flaws like the yips is just a well-designed drill away.

I'VE SPENT THE last 25 years or so of my life investigating the putting stroke—the hows and whys of getting the ball into the hole on a consistent basis. Ultimately, this research spawned the creation of the SAM PuttLab, the industry standard for digitally analyzing putting setups and strokes. As co-inventor of this machinery, I was intent on developing means to break down the stroke to its finite parts to locate commonalities among golfers with good putting strokes and those who struggle. The PuttLab computes 28 different measurements continuously during the stroke. There isn't an acceleration point or wrist angle change that I don't know about.

Over the years I've analyzed 50,000 putting strokes digitally in labs across the globe. To put this number in perspective, it would take you approximately 16 and a half years, playing twice a week, to roll that many putts. Much of my research on this data is geared toward pinpointing areas that lead to poor putting—physical glitches that are impossible to overcome during the short time frame of the stroke. Many of these are easy to fix. Others, like choking, freezing and the yips, require a bit more work, which is why these types of faults tend to stay with you for a while. Like the old saying goes, "If you've ever had the yips, then you have them." These are damaging putting states that go beyond the standard rota of fixes scattered throughout the rest of this book. You need a whole mind-body workout—some of these mistakes are rooted in your body and some of them are rooted in your mind. Either way, I have a cure. Let's get started.

**5 Things I'll Teach You In This Chapter**

**1** The difference between rotational and acceleration yips.

**2** How to cure either type of yip with drills that anyone can perform.

**3** The link between physical errors and mental roadblocks.

**4** Why you sometimes freeze over a putt, and how to get out of the habit.

**5** How to perform under pressure without choking.

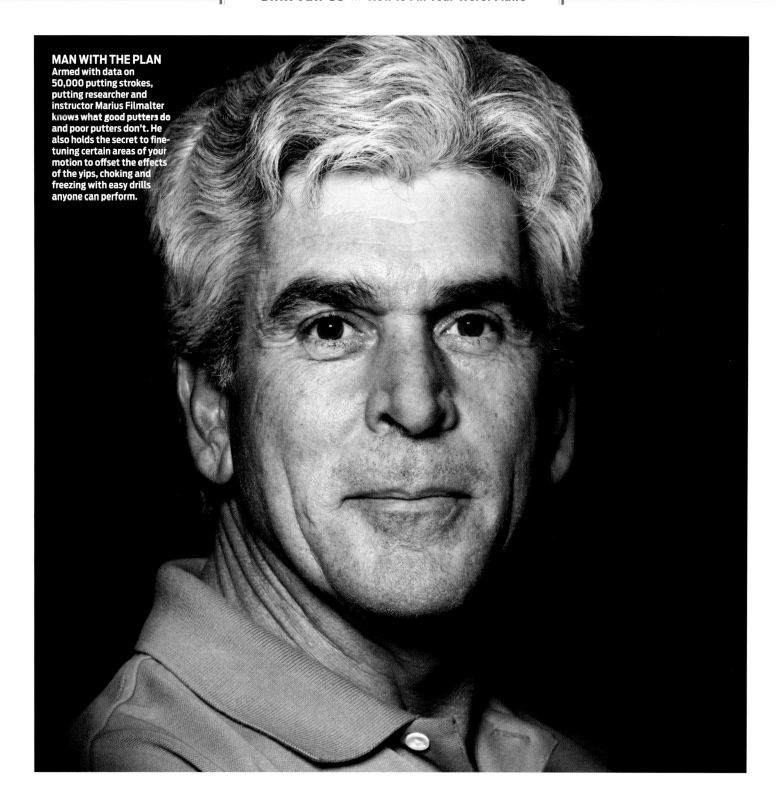

**MAN WITH THE PLAN**
Armed with data on 50,000 putting strokes, putting researcher and instructor Marius Filmalter knows what good putters do and poor putters don't. He also holds the secret to fine-tuning certain areas of your motion to offset the effects of the yips, choking and freezing with easy drills anyone can perform.

### ALL ABOUT ME

**Name:** Marius Filmalter
**Facility:** Marius Golf, Dallas, Tex.
**Teaching since:** 1982
**Where I've taught:** Beurberg C.C., Munich, Germany
**Where I've performed research:** Hank Haney Golf Academy (McKinney, Tex.), Ludwig Maximilian University, Munich, Germany
**Who I've instructed:** Tiger Woods, Ernie Els, Vijay Singh, Trevor Immelman, Y.E. Yang, Ryan Palmer and Jerry Kelly, among 30 other PGA Tour professionals
**Awards I've won:** *Golf Magazine* Innovator Award (2009)
**My best contribution to the game:** Co-inventor of the SamPutt Lab and the TOMI, the industry standards for digital stroke analysis and research; SUPERTEE short-game instruction system, the only machine developed specifically to cure the yips
**For more instruction:** golf.com/bestputtingbook
mariusgolf.com
supertee.com

## "When you start changing the way you think about putting, the results are quick and, most times, quite dramatic."

**F**REEZING. CHOKING. THE YIPS. There isn't a golfer in the world who hasn't either experienced these flaws or shakes in their spikes at their very mention. These are fundamental lapses in putting ability—you're erring in distance, direction *and* feel—and in the case of choking and freezing, incapable of even starting and executing your motion.

For years much of the research on catastrophic flaws such as these focused on the brain—yipping, choking and freezing, to most experts, were mental issues. While there are certainly some mind problems inherent with these flaws, I've learned that you can beat them by improving your physical technique in key areas, and that actually tweaking your motion here and there can trick your mind into performing like normal.

As you read through my tips and drills on the following pages, you'll notice that I won't force you into ultra-specific positions or moves. That's not my style. My whole philosophy on putting isn't to teach people to putt differently, but to think differently. A lot of excellent instructors like to get their students to change the way they putt, but in my opinion that takes too long. It requires practice, and lots of lonely hours on the practice putting green. But when you start changing the way you *think* about putting, the results are quick and, most times, quite dramatic. That's why many of the drills you'll read about in this chapter that deal with hard-

core problems such as yipping, freezing and choking are designed to simply get you into a new state of mind.

The first step in solving any problem is to find out where you are. So if you're a yipper, choker or freezer, fess up. It's okay. We'll fix it. That's the other major tenet I have about putting improvement: In order to get to where you want to be (in this case, to become someone who makes more than their fair share of putts), you must know where you are. That's the beauty of the SAM PuttLab and my other invention, the TOMI. These digital putting analyzers provide a perfect blueprint of your stroke. Come down to my lab in Texas and within minutes I'll tell you how you accelerate, where the putterface is pointing at impact, your angle of approach, the timing of your stroke and 24 other important things that let me know in an instant where you are with your putting game. Building the road from there is easy.

A while back, when Tiger Woods was putting extremely well, he said to me, "Put me on the machine and save the results." Now, we have something to go back to if and when his putting goes awry. It's important to realize that I compare Tiger with himself. Golfers make mistakes when they try to mimic other people's techniques. I don't do that. Everyone is wired differently, everyone stands differently to the ball based on their particular build, and everyone fires their muscles differently and in different sequences. You're psychologically and neurologically unique. A stroke that works for your buddy may not work for you.

There's another benefit to assessing where you are in your putting: you'll probably discover that you're doing a lot of things right in your stroke already. You just need a little direction to weed out the mistakes. Together we'll get to that point. You've admitted that you have the yips (of which there are two kinds; we'll discuss them separately in this chapter), or that you're guilty of choking or freezing (if you don't know for sure, I'll show you how to test yourself for these flaws). That's step one. On to the cures.

### WATCH & LEARN

When you see this icon, go to **golf.com/bestputtingbook** for a free video lesson with Top 100 Teacher Marius Filmalter.

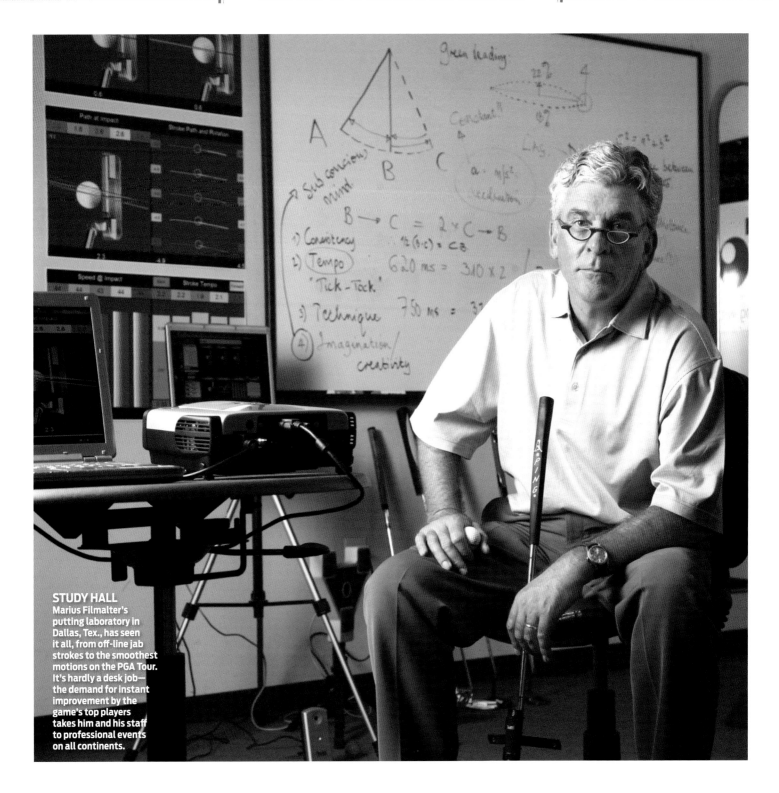

**STUDY HALL**
Marius Filmalter's
putting laboratory in
Dallas, Tex., has seen
it all, from off-line jab
strokes to the smoothest
motions on the PGA Tour.
It's hardly a desk job—
the demand for instant
improvement by the
game's top players
takes him and his staff
to professional events
on all continents.

SPEED RATE

MAX SPEED SHOULD OCCUR HERE

IN A YIP STROKE IT OCCURS HERE

**SPEED ISSUES** Because you think an accelerating stroke is a good stroke, you overdo it and make a jerky forward-stroke past the ball. Good putters accelerate, but they reach top speed before the ball, then maintain it through impact and into their follow-through. This is why good putters' strokes look so smooth.

# FLAW: ACCELERATION YIPS

**ACCELERATION YIPS HAPPEN** when you over-accelerate through impact—that nasty jabbing motion that looks more like you're trying to shoo away a fly than making a putting stroke. Obviously, it's impossible to control distance with this type of yips, which is why sufferers mix coming up short and stabbing the ball way past the hole in equal amounts.

Over-acceleration is a big no-no, but it's not totally your fault if you do it. For years, golfers have been taught to accelerate. You hear it all the time. Maybe you even shout it to yourself when you come up short on an easy uphill putt. This isn't to say that good putters don't accelerate. They do, but there's a huge misunderstanding by the golfing public between acceleration and what's really important—*speed*.

Here's the deal: good putters accelerate up to a certain point, then maintain that speed through the ball. Maintaining speed means there's no acceleration or deceleration. Yippers, on the other hand, are constantly accelerating, and almost always hit max speed after impact.

The best analogy for controlling speed is a car approaching a bridge. You're driving and I'm in the passenger seat. If I asked you to hit the bridge going exactly 60 mph, how would you go about doing it? You wouldn't accelerate all the way up to the bridge and hope you time it right so that you hit 60 right when you get to the bridge. Rather, you'd get to 60 mph as fast as you could, then maintain that rate of speed until you reached the bridge.

My studies with the SAM PuttLab show that good putters reach max acceleration approximately 200 milliseconds before impact (or about an inch to 3 inches behind the ball, depending on stroke speed). What happens in

yipping is that, during your forward-stroke, your mind tells you that you haven't generated enough speed (often because your backstroke is too short—more on that on the opposite page). So you step on the gas and—yip!

## HOW YOU KNOW YOU HAVE THEM

This one's easy. Drop five balls on the green and, using the same stroke length, try to putt each one the same distance. If you have any trouble in completing this task, you're a potential acceleration yipper. Also, if you feel any tension in your arms and hands as you do this drill, you may also be a sufferer. Golfers typically tense up because they think the tenser they are the better chance they have of controlling the putterface. The bad news is that you need tension to accelerate, so you're only adding fuel to the fire.

# WHY IT'S HAPPENING

**ONE OF THE** primary causes of un-needed acceleration is not taking the putter back far enough. It's better to make a longer backstroke than to err on the short side because when your mind senses that you haven't built up enough potential energy to roll the ball the distance you need, it forces you to speed up your stroke.

Ben Crenshaw always said that he liked to take the putter back far enough so that he didn't have to hit the ball. In other words, take it back far enough so that the putter can "float" into impact without any hit effort.

**TRY THIS:** Hold your putter with just your left thumb and forefinger around the top of the grip and out in front of you, and with your right hand pull the putterhead back (like the action on a pendulum). Now let go. Notice that without any effort on your part, the head swings back to its starting position and beyond. It has accelerated—by itself!

The most important thing to know about acceleration yips is that you're doing too much and the putter is doing too little. It's an old cliché, but it holds true: you're getting in your own way.

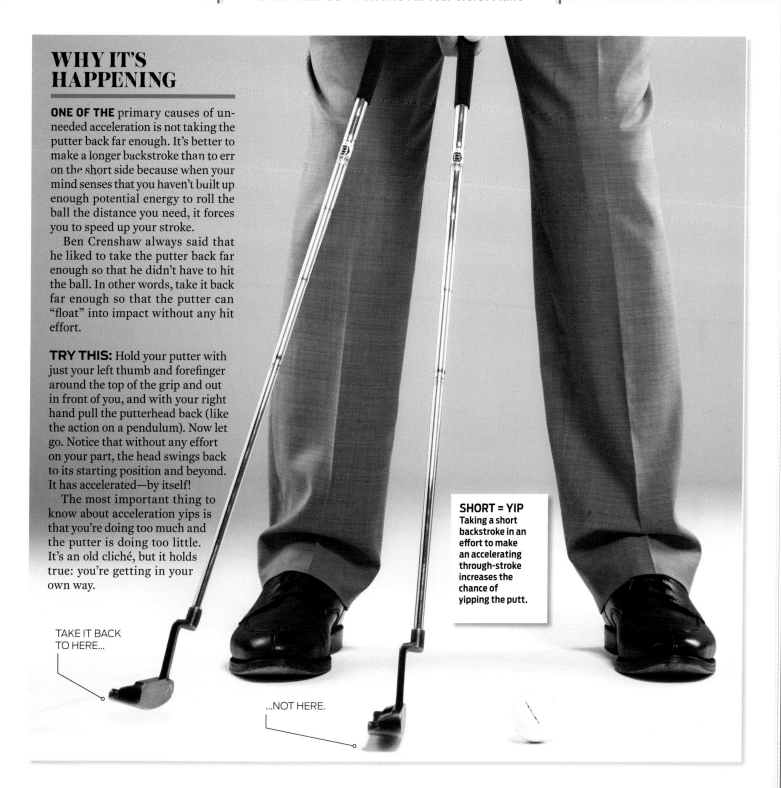

TAKE IT BACK TO HERE...

...NOT HERE.

**SHORT = YIP**
Taking a short backstroke in an effort to make an accelerating through-stroke increases the chance of yipping the putt.

> **"The best fix for an acceleration yipper is to do as little as possible."**

**STEP 1**
Make a few practice continuous strokes over the ball.

**STEP 2**
Without stopping your momentum, swing the head back with the intent to strike the ball.

**STEP 3**
Lower the putter on the way through and hit the putt.

# FIX #1: MAKE A HOVER STROKE

**ONE OF THE** first things I'll have a student who has acceleration yips do is to bring his putter up parallel to the ground and putt an imaginary ball that's at waist height. Without any further instruction they'll make a long backstroke and long through-stroke at a nice easy pace. As soon as I drop a ball on the ground and ask them to putt, however, they go back to their short backstroke and yippy through-stroke. The reason this happens is that most people think of the ball as something that gets in the way. They see it as bigger than it is and heavy—something that needs effort to be moved. As I mentioned previously, the best fix for an acceleration yipper is to do as little as possible.

Try the waist-high putt stroke. Then drop a ball on the ground and, instead of setting your putter behind the ball, hover it above the ball. Make a few practice strokes over the ball [photos, above] and, without stopping your motion, swing the putter back and hit the putt. This blends the free-flowing stroke golfers normally produce without a ball with actual contact. It's one of my best drills.

# FIX #2: THE WOBBLE DRILL

**GRIP YOUR PUTTER** using only your thumbs and forefingers. Place your left hand at the top of the handle and your right hand at the very bottom of the grip. Set up in your normal putting stance and make your stroke (you don't need a ball for this one). If you have any accelerating yip in your stroke, the grip end of the shaft will tilt backward and the putterhead will flip past your hands. The only way to keep the putter from "wobbling" is to maintain constant speed. This is a great drill because the finger hold removes your control of the putter and exposes even the slightest trace of the yips.

Set your thumbs and forefingers lightly on the handle and make your stroke. If you yip, you'll know it—the putterhead will flip past your hands.

YIP          SMOOTH

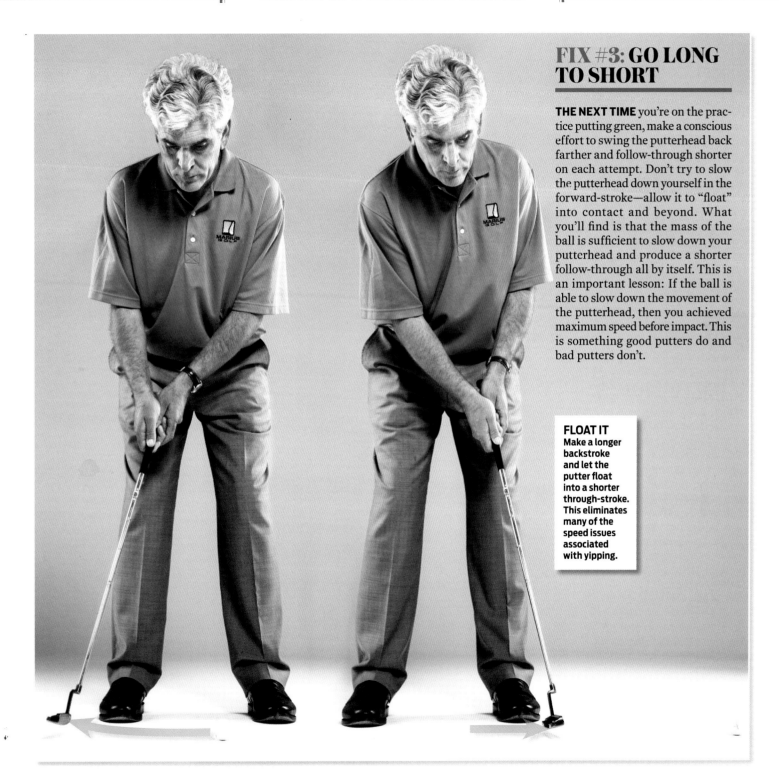

## FIX #3: GO LONG TO SHORT

**THE NEXT TIME** you're on the practice putting green, make a conscious effort to swing the putterhead back farther and follow-through shorter on each attempt. Don't try to slow the putterhead down yourself in the forward-stroke—allow it to "float" into contact and beyond. What you'll find is that the mass of the ball is sufficient to slow down your putterhead and produce a shorter follow-through all by itself. This is an important lesson: If the ball is able to slow down the movement of the putterhead, then you achieved maximum speed before impact. This is something good putters do and bad putters don't.

**FLOAT IT**
Make a longer backstroke and let the putter float into a shorter through-stroke. This eliminates many of the speed issues associated with yipping.

# FLAW: ROTATIONAL YIPS

**THIS FORM OF YIPS** is closely related to acceleration yips, but it's definitely its own distinct flaw. Acceleration yips create problems in distance; rotational yips create problems in *direction*. The way they relate has to do with the way your brain computes information. It's smart, that cranium of yours. It wants to square your putter-face at the moment you reach top speed because it assumes that's when you should strike the ball (and it's correct in thinking this way). However, if your acceleration is off and you don't reach top speed until after impact (acceleration yips), then your putterface will be open when you strike the ball. Your mind hasn't squared it yet because you haven't reached top speed. Not good.

What happens in this scenario is that you set up a battle between your subconscious and conscious minds. Your subconscious mind senses that the face is open too close to impact (at a point where it thinks it should be closing) and reacts by closing it. However, your conscious mind thinks it's already square, so you fight it and open the face. The problem is that it takes approximately 200 milliseconds to transfer a subconscious thought to your conscious self, which is an eternity when you're dealing with something as short as the forward-stroke. The time lag forces a quick-twitch reaction in a last ditch effort to open the face. Thus, the rotational yip, and why the end of this stroke appears so violent and spastic.

This is a pretty heady explanation, so here's an easier way to

**OPEN FACE**
If you don't reach top speed prior to impact, your subconscious will keep the face open.

**CLOSED FACE**
Your conscious mind reacts. It senses the face is open and shuts it.

**REACTION**
Your subconscious fights it—it thinks you're squaring the face early, before you reach top speed.

**YIP!**
The lag time for your conscious mind to respond forces a fast-twitch response, and you jut the face open and to the right.

think about it: The battle between your subconscious and conscious is the same thing as saying that you have doubt about what you're doing. When you have doubt you almost always do things faster. When you're stuck in the woods and need a low draw to escape, it almost never works out because you're unsure of your ability. Your response is to rush your motion. Same thing happens on the green.

## HOW YOU KNOW YOU HAVE ROTATIONAL YIPS

Drop some balls on the green and try putting using only your right hand. Make it a flat 8- to 10-footer. If you can, run a chalk line or a string from the ball to the cup. As you putt balls with your right hand only, assess your ability to start the ball on line and roll it into the cup. If you don't hit it perfect every time it doesn't mean you have rotational yips, but if you really struggle to start the ball on line and keep it there, and you miss more putts than you make, then you're a definite candidate.

> "When you have doubt you almost always do things faster."

# THERE'S MORE THAN ONE WAY TO YIP ROTATIONALLY

**ON THE PREVIOUS** pages I described the typical rotational yip, where you make a list-ditch effort to open the face and end up with the putterface wide open and pushed out to the right. This isn't the only type of rotational yip. A less common but equally damaging scenario happens when your subconscious senses that your putterface is open prior to impact. You respond by closing the face, but then your mind tells you that you haven't closed it enough, so at the last moment you flip the putterhead past your hands, toe over heel, to the left of the target line. This time, the ball shoots to the left of where you're aimed, but the motion is the same: hurried, jerky, and not very pretty. This rotational yip stems from trying to overcontrol the position of the clubface.

**TRANSITION**
Your mind senses that the putterface is open as you start forward.

**REACTION**
Your mind adjusts for the perceived open face by unduly closing it.

**BATTLE**
Your subconscious doesn't like this, so it rotates the face open again.

**YIP!**
Your conscious mind responds by jerking the face and head left of the target

## WHY IT'S HAPPENING

**THE COMMON THREAD** linking both types of rotational yips is, you guessed it, rotation. While it appears that you're using too much of it (what with the putterface opening and closing wildly as your subconscious and unconscious do battle during your stroke), the truth is that you can't simply remove it and solve your rotational yip problems. I'm sorry to burst your bubble, but every putting stroke needs arc, even one that's designed to move straight back and through. Human movement is engineered to move in circles, and most forms of energy are created with centrifugal force. Plus, you're standing next to the ball, not behind it, and your putter is tilted away from pure vertical. This produces an arc naturally, and when you try to fight it, your subconscious kicks in and the battle is on. The only way to make a true straight-back-and-through-stroke is to eliminate the angle of the puttershaft and get your eyes and hands over the target line (for more on this type of stroke, see Chapter 5).

You can't escape rotation in putting, so step one is to accept it. Vijay Singh is constantly telling me that he wants as little arc as possible in his stroke. When we get him on the SAM PuttLab he produces more arc with his long putter than most PGA Tour pros do with a standard-length putter. Once you give in to the fact that rotation is not only okay when you putt, but beneficial, you're on your way to fixing the problem for good.

**"I'm sorry to burst your bubble, but every putting stroke features arc."**

**ROTATION ERRORS**
Every stroke features rotation. When you fight it, you set yourself up to yip and strike the ball with an overly closed *[photo, above]* or open face.

**PURE CONTACT**
You'll hit your smoothest putts when you strike the ball with a square putterface. The mistake most people make is trying to keep it square from start to finish.

# FIX #1:
# PUTT TWO BALLS

**SET TWO BALLS** next to each other on the putting green and position your putter behind them. One of the balls should be closer to the heel and one of them should be closer to the toe. Now make your regular stroke. If the ball nearer the heel travels farther than the ball closer to the toe, then you yipped the putt rotationally. There's no way the heel can rotate past the toe unless you yip. This actually breaks every law in any golf stroke, whether you're making it with your wedges, woods or irons. Your clubs aren't designed to be swung that way. You have a problem.

Keep at this drill until you can make the ball near the toe travel farther than the one near the heel. When this happens, it's evidence that the toe is moving faster than the heel by rotating around it. Get comfortable with this situation—this is the way a good putting stroke works.

**WARNING:** Don't simply rotate your hands to spin the toe past the heel. Your putter doesn't rotate on its own axis. It rotates in relation to the target line, tracing an arc back and through. While the face opens and closes in relation to a straight line to the target, it remains square to the arc from start to finish (for more detail on the arc nature of putting strokes, see Chapter 4).

## "Don't rotate your hands to spin the toe past the heel."

**YES!**
When you correctly trace an arc with your putter, the toe moves faster than the heel, causing the ball farthest from you to travel farther than the one closest to you.

**NO!**
If the ball that's closer to the heel goes farther, you yipped. You forced the heel to rotate past the toe.

# FIX #2:
## MAKE A CHANGE

**ONE OF THE** first things I do with a student who's suffering from rotational yips is to change their grip. Their current grip may be absolutely perfect, but it's more about the change than the hold itself. Making a change like this gives you a clean slate—the chance to tap a different part of your brain. This is a good thing since the part you're using now isn't producing very good results. Clean slates erase the mistakes you've been making, turning past experiences into *passed* experiences. You're on to something new, something you don't have to fight because you don't know what you're going to get. Trust me—it's a powerful feeling.

Mark O'Meara paid me a visit back in early 2004. He wasn't putting well, and he knew it. I showed him the claw grip and asked him to try it. His first response was, "Marius, I'll quit playing golf before I use that grip!" I convinced him to roll one ball with it. His stroke was perfect. He asked for another ball. Then another. Three weeks later he won the Dubai Desert Classic and hasn't changed his grip since.

**PRO PROOF**
A new grip—one he had no interest in trying—gave Mark O'Meara the clean slate he needed to improve his putting and get back in the win column.

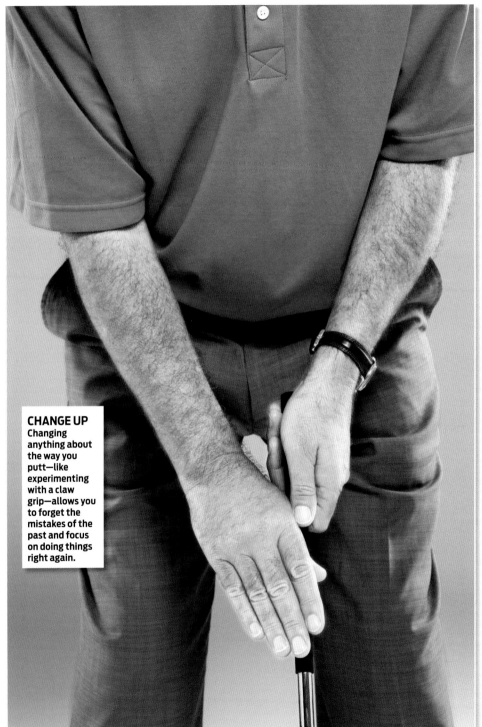

**CHANGE UP**
Changing anything about the way you putt—like experimenting with a claw grip—allows you to forget the mistakes of the past and focus on doing things right again.

# FIX #3: ANTICIPATION DRILL

**PREVIOUSLY, I TALKED** about how most yippers think of the ball as an impediment or as something they have to move instead of simply letting it get in the way, and how removing the ball immediately produces a smoother stroke. It's true—golfers only yip when there's a ball on the ground. Try this drill and prove it to yourself.

Set up to putt and have a friend place his finger on top of the ball *[photos, right]*. Your friend's job is two-fold: to keep the ball where it is on some strokes, and on others, to pull it back just before impact. His goal is to basically surprise you by allowing you to make contact with the ball or not. What happens after a while is that you'll get frustrated ("Is he going to move that damn ball or isn't he?"). Then you'll stop caring ("I don't give a damn what he does, I'm just going to make my stroke."). That's the breakthrough you're looking for. At that point, and it usually takes 25 to 30 balls for the light to turn on, you'll find that you're actually making nice, yip-less putting strokes. You've successfully lost the anticipation of impact. The ball is no longer getting in the way.

**"It's true—golfers only yip when there's a ball on the ground."**

**STEP 1**
Ask a friend to randomly pull the ball back just before impact or leave it.

**STEP 2**
By moving the ball or keeping it in place, your friend is helping you to lose your anticipation of impact.

**RESULT**
Not knowing whether the ball will be there at impact or not teaches you to forget the ball and simply make your stroke.

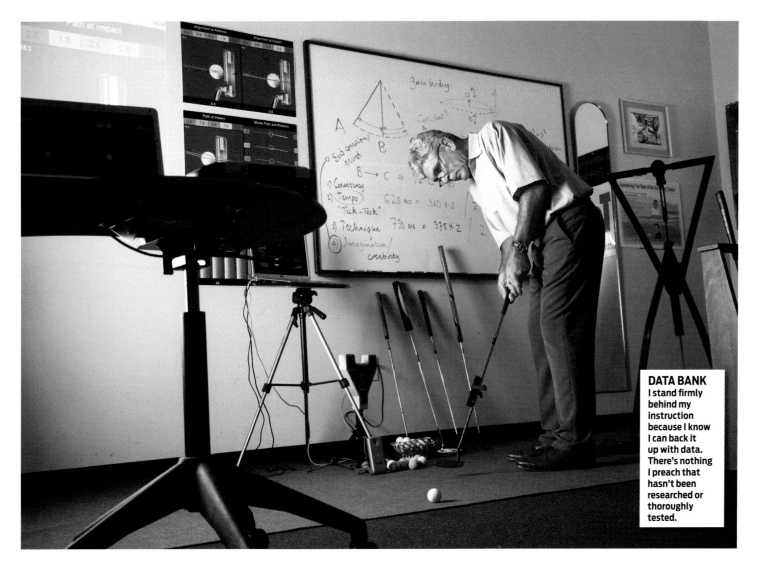

**DATA BANK**
I stand firmly behind my instruction because I know I can back it up with data. There's nothing I preach that hasn't been researched or thoroughly tested.

# BETTER PUTTING THROUGH BETTER RESEARCH

**ONE OF THE** things that's so great about teaching in today's world is the technology—we can see things about your full swing and putting stroke that previous instructors could never dream of, thanks to the modern wave of high-tech devices and specialty computer programs. I was fortunate enough to be part of the team that invented the SAM PuttLab and the TOMI (a sized-down version of the PuttLab that's a little more user friendly and portable). There isn't an ounce of instruction in this chapter that I can't back up with hard data from research using these two machines. I'm a big believer, obviously, in technology's role in instruction. To me it makes all the difference in the world. Sure, a lot of what I do, especially with my Tour students, is very hands on, but when it comes down to demystifying the stroke, there's no friend better than a good piece of hardware.

Take, for example, the drill at left. I've invented a machine called SUPERTEE which basically replicates the role of your buddy during the drill. The machine randomly sets a ball at address, allows you to hit it or makes it disappear. What we found is that the benefits of this type of training works with the full swing as well. For information (and to watch a number of videos of the SUPERTEE in action), visit www.supertee.com.

# FREEZING

**REMEMBER SERGIO GARCIA** in the late 1990s and early 2000s when he couldn't stop gripping and regripping his club? One time I counted 23 regrips before he hit a mid-iron. To me this is the ultimate example of freezing, but it's more commonly experienced on the green where you're over the putt and you just can't *seem... to...pull...the...trigger.*

When you freeze over a putt, you know what the program is (your stroke), but you just can't initiate it. While researchers haven't nailed the specific reasons why we sometimes freeze in a motor action, I strongly suspect that it's because we're not sure of the outcome or that we want to avoid the outcome all together. Either way, it's a serious problem.

Good putters pull the trigger within a specific cycle, which is made up of the steps you take as soon as you start reading your putt *[see examples, right].* Once they complete their cycle, they go. John Daly, for example, has a quick cycle. He reads the putt, steps in, then putts. Other players read the putt, step in, look at the hole, look down and then go. Regardless, it's important to know that the cycle exists because messing with your cycle—or not knowing you have one—leads to freezing.

**1** **2** **3**

**QUICK!** Only a handful of golfers can make a solid stroke with a 3-step cycle.

**7** **8**

**LOST** Shuffling in your stance like this so deep into your cycle is not a good sign.

**9**

**PERFECT**
My research shows that a 5-step cycle works for most players.

*The three most important things about cycles are:*

**1. The longer your cycle, the greater the chance that you'll freeze.** This happens because as you grind over a putt you continue to feed your brain with information, and the more information your brain has to filter, the less likely it will make an efficient decision, especially when you know you're on the clock.

**2. Once you pass the end of your cycle, you must wait for it to restart.** This just adds to the anguish as you stand over the ball.

**3. Regardless of how many steps are in your cycle, pull the trigger on the same step every time.**

## TRIGGER HAPPY

As you can imagine, a lot of this deals with developing a solid pre-putt routine that you know by heart and that you trust. It also deals with developing a trigger. A lot of the great putters on Tour can't start their putting stroke without counting in their head, forward-pressing their hands or even lifting their big toe. These seemingly meaningless movements are often necessary for the player to jump-start the action—to force them to act at the right moment in their cycle. If you find yourself freezing over putts, develop a trigger. You'll be in good company.

**FROZEN!**
If you haven't pulled the trigger within 10 steps, you're frozen.

**OUCH**
This putt has no chance.

**AARON BADDELEY**
His quick-step putting cycle
is a good one to copy.

## FIX #1:
## SUCCESSION DRILL

**LINE UP NINE** balls on the green as shown. Step into the first one, look at the hole, then putt. As soon as the ball is on its way, step to the next ball and, without looking at the cup, make your stroke. Then do it again and again until you've hit all nine balls. Don't worry about where the ball is going—just continuously step to the next ball and make your stroke. Your goal here is to develop a quicker cycle, which is a good thing because longer cycles are more apt to end in freezing. After a couple of turns with this drill, perform the entire cycle (step, look, putt) with each ball. Ingrain the cycle and take it to the course.

**PUTT & GO**
Hitting balls
in succession
helps speed
up your cycle
so you can
putt without
freezing.

# FIX #2:
# TAP DRILL

**FOR THIS ONE** you'll need your trusty friend again. Set up to putt with your friend next to you. The trick here is that you can't start your stroke until your friend taps you on the shoulder. You must wait for the command, which is exactly what you're missing if you're a freezer. The tap on your shoulder is the password to initiate your program. Mission accomplished—you have a physical command to replace the mental one that's missing.

I know what you're saying—"I can't do this on the course." You can, in a way. Many of my students ring me after a round and tell me, "I know you weren't playing with us today, but I could feel your tap on my shoulder."

**WAIT FOR IT**
Don't putt until you feel the tap.

**THEN GO**
The tap gives you a physical cue to replace the mental one you're missing.

# FIX #3:
# 5-STEP PUTT

**THIS ONE IS** simple but effective. If you're a freezer, you need to putt more like Aaron Baddeley does. He steps in, spreads his feet, looks at the hole, then the ball, and then he putts. Try his cycle on for size. Set up and then count the steps in your head as you execute them. You can even count out loud. When you first look down, count "1." Count "2" as you look back to the ball, and so on. Build some tempo into the cycle. You should complete each step in rhythmic time (i.e., don't jump from one step to the next faster or slower than you do for the others). The five-frame cycle is ideal. Anything less than that and you're probably not giving the putt your best effort; anything longer than 5 is treading toward freeze territory.

**COUNT "1"**
Step in.

**COUNT "2"**
Take your stance.

**COUNT "3"**
Look at your target.

**COUNT "4"**
Look back at the ball.

**"5"**
Pull the trigger.

# CHOKING

**YOU'RE ON THE** range. You're striping it with every club in your bag. You make your way to the first tee and proceed to top your drive. What happened? In a word, you choked. You initiated the program, but the program didn't function.

We all remember Greg Norman at the 1996 Masters, where he entered the final round leading by six shots over Nick Faldo and ended up losing by seven. Norman had his program on cruise control all week. He knew what to do. On Sunday, however, he had the ability to execute his program (he wasn't freezing), but the program went haywire.

Choking can happen anywhere, but most of the time it rears its head on the putting green because, let's face it, that's where the pressure is. When you miss on your drive or your approach, you know that there's still a chance to make up for the stroke with a good chip or bunker shot. When you miss a putt, you know that the stroke is gone forever.

Greg Norman choked because he felt this pressure. He wanted that Green Jacket. Pressure is the conduit to choking. It can come from an internal source ("I need this putt to win this skin") or an external source (water between you and your target, or a stiff breeze). Wherever the pressure comes from, it has the ability to cause you to misfire your program and choke.

The interesting thing about choking is that it isn't all in your mind. Pressure causes tension. Tension causes your muscles to move slower. You physically react to your perceived sense of angst. That's where the misfire comes from.

## HOW TO NOT BE A CHOKE ARTIST

To alleviate pressure you have to alleviate the tension. Here are some easy ways to stay calm and keep choking at bay.

**DON'T GIVE UP!**
The key is to beating pressure is to gauge your personality to see if you're ready to fight it or roll with it.

**1. BREATHE**
Pressure causes your muscles to tense and move slower. A slower muscle needs more oxygen than a fast one. So, you guessed it, breathe. Take deep breaths as you walk from one shot to the next. Hold each breath for a count and then slowly exhale. This is a proven tension fighter.

**2. DRINK**
Along these same lines, drink lots of water out on the course. This is another way to increase the oxygen uptake by your body.

**3. EAT**
Properly nourishing yourself before and even during play is critical.

**4. EXERCISE**
Perform exercises during your round. I'm not asking you to do pushups between holes, but soft knee bends and toe touches a few times during your round are a healthy way to stay calm and relaxed.

**5. BUILD A KILLER INSTINCT**
Instead of taking steps to fight pressure, some players invite it. Jack Nicklaus and Tiger Woods are two guys who learned to see pressure as a positive and to build it into their overall game plan, to the extent that they likely don't perform as well in the absence of pressure.

**6. LAUGH IT AWAY**
If you don't think you can stare pressure down, then brush it aside. When you feel it, start up a conversation with your foursome. Tell a joke or whistle a tune. Lee Trevino did this all the time—a completely different approach than the track Tiger and Jack take, but nonetheless effective.

**GOLF** MAGAZINE

**EDITOR**
David M. Clarke

**CREATIVE DIRECTOR**
Paul Crawford

**EXECUTIVE EDITOR**
Eamon Lynch

**ART DIRECTOR**
Paul Ewen

**MANAGING EDITORS**
David DeNunzio (Instruction),
Gary Perkinson (Production),
Robert Sauerhaft (Equipment)

**EDITOR AT LARGE**
Connell Barrett

**DEPUTY MANAGING EDITOR**
Michael Chwasky (Instruction & Equipment)

**SENIOR EDITORS**
Alan Bastable, Joseph Passov (Travel/Course
Rankings), Michael Walker Jr.

**DEPUTY ART DIRECTOR**
Karen Ha

**PHOTO EDITORS**
Carrie Boretz (Associate),
Jesse Reiter (Assistant)

**SENIOR WRITER**
Cameron Morfit

**ASSOCIATE EDITOR**
Steven Beslow

**ASSISTANT EDITOR**
Jessica Marksbury

**PUBLISHER**
Dick Raskopf

**ASSOCIATE ADVERTISING DIRECTOR**
Nathan Stamos

**DIRECTOR OF BUSINESS DEVELOPMENT**
Brad J. Felenstein

**GENERAL MANAGER**
Peter Greer

**BUSINESS DEVELOPEMENT MANAGER**
Russ Vance

**HUMAN RESOURCES DIRECTOR**
Liz Mattila

Time HOME ENTERTAINMENT

**EDITOR, SPORTS ILLUSTRATED GROUP**
Terry McDonell

**MANAGING EDITOR, SI.COM**
Paul Fichtenbaum

**MANAGING EDITOR, SI GOLF GROUP**
James P. Herre

**PRESIDENT, CORPORATE SALES & MARKETING**
Leslie Picard

**PRESIDENT, TIME INC. MEDIA GROUP**
Wayne Powers

**PRESIDENT, DIGITAL**
Kirk McDonald

**V.P., CONSUMER MARKETING**
John Reese

**V.P., COMMUNICATIONS**
Scott Novak

**V.P., GENERAL MANAGER, SI DIGITAL**
Ken Fuchs

**NEWS GROUP**

**PRESIDENT & GROUP PUBLISHER**
Mark Ford

**SENIOR V.P. & GROUP GENERAL MGR.**
Andy Blau

**SENIOR V.P., DIGITAL**
John Cantarella

**GOLF.com**

**EXECUTIVE EDITOR**
Charlie Hanger

**EXECUTIVE PRODUCER**
Christopher Shade

**DEPUTY EDITOR**
David Dusek

**SENIOR PRODUCERS**
Ryan Reiterman, Jeff Ritter

**ASSOCIATE ART DIRECTOR**
Omar Sharif

**SR. AD OPERATIONS MANAGER**
Elise LeScoezec

**PUBLISHER**
Richard Fraiman

**GENERAL MANAGER**
Steven Sandonato

**EXECUTIVE DIRECTOR, MARKETING SERVICES**
Carol Pittard

**DIRECTOR, RETAIL & SPECIAL SALES**
Tom Mifsud

**DIRECTOR, NEW PRODUCT DEVELOPMENT**
Peter Harper

**DIRECTOR, BOOKAZINE DEVELOPMENT & MARKETING**
Laura Adam

**PUBLISHING DIRECTOR, BRAND MARKETING**
Joy Butts

**ASSISTANT GENERAL COUNSEL**
Helen Wan

**DESIGN & PREPRESS MANAGER**
Anne-Michelle Gallero

**BOOK PRODUCTION MANAGER**
Susan Chodakiewicz

**ASSOCIATE BRAND MANAGER**
Allison Parker

**THE BEST PUTTING INSTRUCTION BOOK EVER!**
by the *GOLF Magazine* Putting Instructors
with David DeNunzio

**DESIGN**
Paul Ewen

**PHOTOGRAPHY**
Angus Murray (Instruction),
Schecter Lee (Equipment)
Getty Images (pp. 106-107, 171, 176)

**IMAGING**
Geoffrey A. Michaud (Director, SI Imaging)
Dan Larkin, Robert M. Thompson, Gerald Burke

**PROJECT EDITORS**
David DeNunzio, Alan Bastable,
Michael Chwasky, Michael Corcoran

**COPY EDITOR**
Gary Perkinson

**VIDEO PRODUCTION**
John Ledesma/Optimism Media Group

**The best lessons from *GOLF Magazine* and the Top 100 Teachers in America!**

Learn the fastest ways to improve your scores with our *Best!* series of instruction manuals. For more information, visit **golf.com/instruction**.

## 1
*The Best Instruction Book Ever!*
**The ultimate how-to guide for improving every part of your game and every moment of your swing.**

## 2
*How to Hit Every Shot*
**Expert advice on how to shape shots and beat anything the course throws at you.**

## 3
*The Best Short Game Instruction Book Ever!*
**Over 100 ways to chip, pitch, blast and wedge your way close from 100 yards and in.**

## 4
*The Best Little Instruction Book Ever!*
**Pocket-sized tips for complete game improvement from the Top 100 Teachers in America.**

**THANK YOU!**

Alexandra Bliss, Glenn Buonocore, Jim Childs, Caroline DeNunzio, F. David DeNunzio, Harvey Ewen, Lauren Hall, Malena Jones, Suzanne Janso, Brynn Joyce, Robert Marasco, Amy Migliaccio, Kimberely Posa, Brooke Reger, Ilene Schrieder, Adrianna Tierno, Alex Voznesenskiy, Sydney Webber.

# GOLF
## MAGAZINE

## Enjoy
# 6 FREE ISSUES!

GOLF Magazine is the leading authority on the game of golf.
Receive instruction tailored to your game, tournament coverage, articles
on travel and lifestyle, and equipment advice from the Pro's.

# 6 FREE ISSUES R.S.V.P.

**YES!** Send me 12 issues of GOLF Magazine – PLUS 6 more issues absolutely FREE!
That's a total of 18 monthly issues in all for the special low rate of just $12. If I don't enjoy
the magazine, I can cancel at any time and receive a full refund on all unmailed issues.

NAME _____ (PLEASE PRINT)

ADDRESS _____

CITY STATE ZIP _____

EMAIL ADDRESS _____

☐ Bill me later.     GFANXX6

**TEEING OFF:** Pictorial presentation of the game.

**THE STARTER:** Interviews with Tour stars, instruction from Dave Pelz, guide to the rules, special swing sequences of players in form.

**YOUR GAME:** The *Golf* magazine Top 100 Teachers In America share their knowledge to give quick tips to improve.

**THE *GOLF* MAGAZINE INTERVIEW:** In-depth questioning of the player of the moment.

**THE SHOP:** Latest golf equipment showcase.

**SIDESPIN:** David Feherty's hilarious take on the game.

**FEATURE ARTICLES:** Major profiles of the best players in the world, previews of the majors, behind-the-scenes of the PGA Tour.

SEND
BACK TODAY
FOR YOUR
**6 FREE**
ISSUES